UNARMED

UNARMED
An American Educator's Memoir

Megan Doney

Washington Writers' Publishing House
Washington, DC

COVER DESIGN by Andrew Sargas Klein
BOOK DESIGN and TYPOGRAPHY by Barbara Shaw

Cornflake Girl: Words and Music by Tori Amos
Copyright © 1993 Sword And Stone Publishing, Inc. (ASCAP)
International Copyright Secured   All Rights Reserved
Reprinted by Permission of Music Sales Corporation
Reprinted by Permission of Hal Leonard LLC

Disclaimer

This is a memoir and reflects the author's present recollections of experiences over time. Some names and identifying details have been changed; some conversations have been compressed and recreated. The views expressed here are solely the author's own.

ISBN 978-1-94155-41-71
Library of Congress Control Number: 2024939096

Printed in the United States of America

WASHINGTON WRITERS' PUBLISHING HOUSE
2814 5th Street NE, #1301
Washington, DC 20017
More information: www.washingtonwriters.org

DC COMMISSION ON THE ARTS & HUMANITIES

maryland state arts council

Support for Washington Writers' Publishing House comes from the DC Commission on the Arts & Humanities and the Maryland State Arts Council

PROUD MEMBER

[clmp]

COMMUNITY OF LITERARY MAGAZINES & PRESSES
W W W . C L M P . O R G

I WOULD LIKE TO DEDICATE THIS BOOK

To every one of my students, with whom I have been privileged to learn, laugh, and cry.

To the cherished memory of Sara Logan and Fr. David McIlhiney, who believed me and believed in me.

And to Johan.

GRATEFUL ACKNOWLEDGMENT is made to the following publications in which sections of this book first appeared in essay form: *Ilanot Review,* "Men Appear as Monsters," *Rappahannock Review,* "Sweet, Quiet Boys; or, Divinities Implacable," *New Limestone Review,* "Ice Is a Rock That Flows," and *Creative Nonfiction,* "The Wolf and the Dog."

Contents

By their laughter I know my students
hear the voices of an unarmed choir. We teach
peace in the stuttering light, reconcile silence
with the world's residual, clamorous beauty.

—Lucinda Roy, "End Words: A Sestina"

Prologue

March 13, 1996

ON THIS DAY, all over the world, millions of people are walking: to catch a train or subway, to exercise their dogs, to get to school or work.

On this day, a man in a small town in central Scotland is walking. As he nears a school parking lot, he cuts the phone lines that serve the adjacent neighborhood. He is carrying four guns, all legally acquired: two 9mm pistols and two .357 Magnum revolvers. Inside the school, a Primary 1 class is having gym.

On this day, I am walking home from my classes at the University of Aberdeen, a city on the North Sea about two hours north of Dunblane, where I am spending a semester abroad. It's my first time outside the United States. I share a flat with one other American student and three Scottish girls. As I enter, I find two of my Scottish flatmates huddled in a bedroom, watching television, their faces swollen and sticky with weeping. The man shot sixteen children dead in that gymnasium in Dunblane, along with one teacher, and injured fifteen others before killing himself.

Later that week, as the country reels and rages, I am walking in Aberdeen's city center when I see a newspaper advertisement pasted on a sign. The headline reads:

THIS SHOULD HAPPEN IN AMERICA, NOT HERE.

I'm indignant. *It shouldn't happen anywhere*, I think to myself. *Don't blame America.* 1996 is before Jonesboro, Arkansas; before Paducah, Kentucky; before Pearl, Mississippi; and before Littleton, Colorado, which will finally launch the United States into an era when school shootings become a familiar aberration.

Later that semester, the coordinators for my study abroad program take all of us on a trip to the Highlands. I am stunned by the landscapes, the enormity of the sky, the whistling silences. We stop, of course, at Loch Ness. When I was in the second grade, our student teacher, Miss Wheeler, assigned us to write fan letters to the Loch Ness Monster. I have no idea how she came up with this task, but since I still remember it forty years later, it seems a positive indication of her pedagogical skill. Or else it's just evidence that even as a small girl, I had a predilection for the eldritch and weird.

From Urquhart Castle, that iconic ruin on the shores of the loch, I gaze out at the water. The loch is a long, thin rift in the Great Glen, and it holds more water than all the lakes in England and Wales combined. Peat clouds the water, making visibility extremely low. I cannot see from one end of the lake to the other. Length and depth alike, unfathomable. I think of this, now, nearly thirty years later: about perspectives, limitations, the human inability to see more than an inch in front of us.

I think now about that headline, THIS HAPPENS IN AMERICA. What did the British know about us?

An article in *Smithsonian* magazine quotes British criminologist Peter Squires: "'The notion that someone would use handguns to kill children, like shooting fish in a barrel, was just so appalling that it provoked a reaction beyond that which had been experienced with Hungerford,' a 1987 massacre that left 16 adults in a small English town dead and 15 others seriously injured."

After the massacre at Dunblane, the Conservative-led government heeded public calls for gun control and passed the Firearms Amendment Act of 1997, which banned high-caliber handguns and restricted certain other handguns to use only in licensed clubs.

Because it had happened once before, there were no cries of governmental overreach, no insistence that this was a one-off black swan event.

In April 2013, mere months after the massacre of twenty-six children and teachers at Sandy Hook Elementary School in Newtown, Connecticut, the U.S. Senate voted down expanded background checks on gun purchases.

Because it had happened dozens of times before, there were cries of governmental overreach, insistence that this was a one-off black swan event.

I'm often asked what I feel hopeful about, in the realm of gun violence prevention. The word *hope*: "Old English *hopian* 'have the theological virtue of Hope; hope for (salvation, mercy), trust in (God's word),' also 'to have trust, have confidence; assume confidently or trust' (that something is or will be so), a word of unknown origin."

Instead of hope, I think of possibility. I try to remember that different choices are possible. The British people and government saw a gymnasium full of dead children and said *never again*. The UK has had one mass shooting since 1996.

I try to remember that instead of *sending thoughts and prayers don't politicize a tragedy it's not the right time to talk about gun control*, leaders might say *I will honor your life and your loved one's life by making sure no one suffers in this way ever again*. I try to remember that the Second Amendment was not always sacred. I try to remember that countries and cultures can course-correct, rewrite their founding documents, welcome necessary change, and accept the humility that comes with acknowledging failure. I try to remember that throughout history, people have strived and learned and lost face and regained it so that they would leave a better world for the generations to come. I try to remember that words are beautiful and powerful, and will always be there when I need them.

Everything is a choice.

Email to my now-husband, December 15, 2012, the day after Sandy Hook:

> I love my work. I love being a teacher. It's the best of me that I can give, to my students. But this makes me even more scared to go to work than I already am sometimes. I hate fearing my own students. But my campus is completely open—one site is in a mall, for God's sake. What chance would I, or any of my students and colleagues have, against someone armed like this and so determined to murder???

Doors

WHEN I TEACH MY STUDENTS how to write strong introductions, I use the metaphor of a door. *Our job as writers is to create a door that's intriguing, welcoming, something that makes our readers so curious that they want to open it, sit down, have some tea, and explore the rest of the house.* I have a few slides of stock photos of front doors, one painted crimson, fringed with flowerbeds and mullioned windows, an entrance to a seemingly enchanted cottage, alongside another that's scrawled with graffiti and hanging off its hinges, revealing a shadowy interior.

The introduction paragraph sets up the conflict, shows us who or what we should care about, I remind them. *How can we ensure our readers will walk through that door and stick with us for the rest of the essay?* You can't move backward through the doors; they only propel forward momentum. There's no return.

Behind Door #1
Friday, April 12, 2013

I am thirty-eight years old and a full-time professor at New River Community College in Virginia. This semester I teach at the satellite campus in Christiansburg, which is in the local shopping mall and occupies the space that was once a movie theater.

The lecture auditoriums still have that feel, with a sloping center aisle and a large screen at the front. I've been separated from my husband, Tom, since October, and this afternoon I have an appointment with a lawyer in town to begin formal divorce proceedings. In a meeting with my therapist three days earlier, I told her that I really felt like I was doing fine.

"I think I'm going to be okay," I said. "I don't think I need to see you every week anymore."

"I agree," she said. "I think you were farther along in the grieving process than you thought you were."

That doesn't mean, however, that the grief doesn't still pound me or that I'm always proud of how I handle things. To my shame, I spend part of my lunch break googling my soon-to-be-ex-husband's affair partner, and send a woeful email to my best friends. I'm sick of her, of him, of the space they both continue to occupy in my mind. But my father is coming to visit me tonight, stopping on his way to the Outer Banks, and I am looking forward to seeing him. I've left my little house unlocked so that in case he arrives before my workday is over, he can go on in, maybe take my dog for a walk.

My afternoon class is English 112, the second semester of college composition. I love this class. My students are so smart and funny and thoughtful. All of the units in the course are oriented around an inquiry question, and the unit we've just finished asked, "What does it mean to be safe?" We read and discussed the intentions and impacts of drug policy, anti-bullying measures in school, and a recent article from the *Atlantic* arguing for more guns in the hands of civilians. They've just turned in the unit papers, which means I have long days of grading ahead of me. Still, I look forward to reading their work. Being with them is a perfect way to end the week.

We are starting today on the final unit for the semester, in which we're going to interrogate the question "What are our responsibilities to other people?" To begin the unit, I'm going to show a segment from *When the Levees Broke*, Spike Lee's documentary about Hurricane Katrina; we will be reading the *New York Times* article about Memorial Hospital, where some physicians administered lethal doses of painkiller to patients they thought would not survive. I slide my DVD into the machine, queue it up, adjust the volume, and sit in the swivel chair behind the instructor console at the front of the room. The flooded, haunted streets of New Orleans fill the screen.

There is a loud, sharp *bang*.

"What was that?"

One of my students asks this.

It must be a car backfiring, I think.

I rise from my chair at the computer console and walk over to the classroom door. I open it.

Two more shots. I know what they are.

I CLOSE THE DOOR SLIGHTLY, as if to barricade us in, but then I look at the emergency exit, right by our classroom door. The exit is just a few steps away, so close that I could sprint through it in three big leaps. *Funny*, I think, there is a car parked right up at the door, a white car, in my memory something practical and boxy like an older Accord. I do not connect the shots with the car until later, that he parked there, not in the parking lot, to block our exit.

I throw the door open, turn to my students, and say, "Get out."

They fly over the desks and they're gone, through the emergency exit, in an instant. They scatter, run to their cars and screech off, away from campus. Outside, I stand dazed in the April sun, uncomprehending. We're the only ones outside; why isn't everyone pouring out the front doors?

I hear more *bangs* and I wonder if everyone inside is dying.

My student Gavin screams at me to get into his car, and I do, for a moment, while he frantically tries to dial 911. I remember the screen on his phone, that neat grid of numbers, and how he keeps messing it up over and over again, his hand shaking, unable to even get the sequence of those three numbers right. *Holy shit*, he keeps saying over and over. *Holy shit.*

"I have to see what's happening," I tell him, and he reluctantly lets me out.

I walk back toward the main entrances; the college's doors are just to the right of the mall entrance. The white car is still parked in front of the emergency exit, from which we'd just fled moments? hours? ago. It's a Friday afternoon, and there are plenty of other cars in the lot, mall patrons and college staff and students mingled. Still, no one emerges from either set of doors. I cannot figure out why. *Why aren't people coming out? Where is everyone? Why am I the only one out here?* I wonder if I have made a horrific mistake and traumatized my students for no reason; maybe it was just a car backfiring, maybe I panicked and irrevocably fucked this up. In three days, it will be the sixth anniversary of the Virginia Tech massacre in Blacksburg, just down the road, where a student murdered thirty-two people; maybe that was in my subconscious, maybe I overreacted.

I hear three more shots.

Now, I feel fear. The bones in my legs melt and I collapse to the pavement, shaking. Silver confetti glitters at the corners of my vision, threatening to blind me. Lines from an old Tori Amos song float in my head:

> *This is not really, this, this*
> *this is not really happening*
> *You bet your life it is.*

AND THEN the sirens start.

Another student of mine grabs me and tells me *for fuck's sake get behind a car, get inside, hide, don't stand out here* and all of a sudden I'm in a stranger's car, and they hand me their cell phone as I squeeze into their backseat along with a few other kids I recognize but can't name. I struggle to remember any phone numbers, and it occurs to me how stupid this is, how twenty-first century, when everyone carries all their numbers in a phone and doesn't bother to memorize anything anymore. The only number I can think of right away is Tom's, and so even though we're filing for divorce and haven't lived together for six months, I call him.

"There's been a shooting at school. I'm okay. Please get in touch with my sisters and mom on Facebook. I don't know their numbers." He asks if he should come get me. "I don't think you could get near here right now. I'll call you when I know something more." Time seems to have stopped working, a clock on a low battery with a drunken second-hand skittering backwards and forwards, everything taking infinitely long, everything happening in less than a heartbeat.

The women whose car we commandeered wants to leave, and so we get out, huddled together in the sunshine. Police cars race up to the entrance. Someone gets out, holding a gun, aimed at the front doors. Within minutes, a uniformed officer bends a young man I don't recognize over the hood of a police car, cuffing his hands behind him. I hear the low, ground-shaking rhythmic thrum of a helicopter. Someone is being taken to a hospital on the helicopter. That's bad, it must be bad. I watch it land in the parking lot, then take off again.

And then more kids and more faculty come out, the students' faces stunned or blank, their mouths open as they cry and clutch their cell phones to their ears, calling anyone they can think of. They abandon texting for the immediate comfort of hearing a human voice on the other end. A few of my faculty colleagues emerge, some weeping, and I hear how the shooter walked straight into one classroom, stared the students in the face, and fired off three rounds directly at them.

My friend who teaches biology tells me how she barricaded herself in the shared faculty offices. How they pushed a table in front of the door and hid, hearing the shots in the hallway, the insistent clank of someone trying to open the door to the office, the voice saying "Help! Let me in! He's got a gun!" and another professor who said, "Don't let him in, that's the shooter."

I ask who was hurt, is anyone dead, speculating *Did Caren get out? Who was in the lobby? Is Frank all right?* I walk around the crowded parking lot looking for all my kids, trying to account for them, but they scattered so quickly I can't even imagine where they are. I try to do a mental head count. *Did I see them all get out? No*, I realize. I could account for maybe half, but the others I can't place. I want to vomit, and I pray that they just drove away unharmed.

Of course, the media is there already, young reporters barely out of college themselves walking around with expressions of sympathy on their faces but a good grip on their microphones as they ask me if I could tell them what happened. I say *for Christ's sake it just happened five minutes ago I have nothing to say to you*, and they nod sympathetically and move on to a more pliant witness.

HOW LONG DOES IT TAKE for the police to come and clear the scene? I wait in a line to give a statement. I am given a ballpoint pen and a blank pad of paper. Like a stroke victim, I've forgotten how to construct a letter on the page and I sit there dumbly for a few minutes, hearing the people around me saying things like *shock* and *get her something to drink* and *where was she. Who are they talking about*, I wonder.

I put the pen tip to the page and move it, and then words appear in red ink, but they aren't in my usual handwriting. I manage to give them a paragraph, sign and date it. This statement has vanished, I assume, into the galaxy of paperwork that surrounds a school shooting. I have never seen it since. I cannot recall a single word that I wrote, only the flimsy beige barrel of the pen, the red cap, the red ink. It was an unsatisfying, utilitarian pen. Not what you would want to write with, for something of such magnitude.

ALL OF MY THINGS: laptop, purse, phone, car keys, house keys—everything is inside the classroom, and I can't go to get them. My biology professor friend drives me to her house, and then Tom comes to fetch me and take me home. My father is sitting on my front steps when we pull up; though I left the house unlocked, he hadn't even tried the door. As I stagger out of Tom's truck I see my dad's surprise, and Tom tells him what's happened; no one had managed to get a message to him en route. I watch the men confer. It's the first time they've seen each other since the two of us split up. They hug. Tom tells me to call him at any time for whatever I need.

I don't remember sleeping that night. I must have, because the next night, and the next, and the next, and the next, I won't.

Behind Door #2

Saturday morning. Dad drives me back to campus to see whether I can retrieve my possessions.

There's yellow caution tape around the entrance, and sheaves of plastic sheeting hang in the doorway. They rattle in the wind like ghosts. A student is also waiting. An administrator lets us in, one by one, to get our things. He puts a hand on my arm and calls me "dear." He's already fetched my things from my classroom and the faculty office, but I still have to walk down the hallway to gather everything.

My school is a crime scene.

I see the holes in the walls and doors where the shooter fired at students and staff. There is a bullet hole in the shape of a star in the door to the tiny copy room, where I later learn that a co-worker was shot through the hand as she tried to hide. Computer stations are littered with abandoned cell phones, students' backpacks, notebooks, laptops, as in the aftermath of the Rapture. My book bag and purse and computer case have never felt so heavy.

As Dad and I leave, I start crying in the parking lot. "What am I going to say to them?" I wail. My father, a retired principal, has no reply.

School is closed the following Monday and Tuesday before reopening the campus. On Monday there is a faculty meeting with administrators and counseling staff from Virginia Tech. They are, unfortunately, quite familiar with the aftermath of a school shooting. We are told that if they wish, students can take their grades as they are and finish the semester three weeks early; or, they can continue to come to class, complete work, and sit for their final exams. It doesn't occur to me to ask what will happen if *I* can't come to class.

One administrator reiterates that the official college safety protocol still advises sheltering in place and locking down during an "incident." Even though we might think that we have safe egress, she says, we never know whether there's a second shooter and if we might be sending students into sniper fire.

I think about how quickly I made the decision to tell my students to run that day, once the shots began (*Get out*), how they flew over their desks and out the emergency exit door, how quickly they vanished into their cars and sped away, or hid with me behind parked cars. Gavin, unable to dial 911. I remember the sound of gunfire coming from the reception lobby, just around the corner, and the certainty that it—he—would come closer. The emergency exit was right in front of us. Using it had seemed like the only option. But what I hear from this administrator is that I could have sent my students into a gauntlet of bullets from an unknown second assailant, and that if they are unhurt today, it is in spite of my choices, not because of them.

Images of my students tumbling one by one in a storm of bullets punch me in the gut. I crumple forward in my seat and sob. The administrator comes up to me afterwards and pats me on the back, saying that I did the right thing and that no one is criticizing my choice in the moment. I can't stop crying, though. The thought of my students, dead because of me, is too much to hold.

Tuesday night, I sit at my desk at home, with an open Word document on my laptop. I've been writing lesson plans for fifteen years, but this one flummoxes me. What are my objectives? Do they matter?

There were no lectures in graduate school on how to craft this lesson.

Behind Door #3

On Wednesday, April 17, I drive to work. I have my purse and my school bag and my lunch bag and a piece of paper with the heading "Post-shooting lesson plans."

When I open the doors to the campus I start to cry almost immediately. The site looks just as it always has, before the shooting. No patched paint. The doors are all brand new. No bloodstains on the carpet. Shattered glass has been swept and vacuumed up. The place looks as though nothing happened, but in my mind it's grotesque, broken, surreal, Picasso's

Guernica in a school.

Shot one, pause—
Two, three
Get out

Plastic sheeting, bullet hole in the door to the test vault, blood on the floor, my students' set and terrified faces.

There are people around all day to care for us, counselors and people from the county court system. A police officer is there every day for the rest of the semester. The victim assistance staff assures us that we can access counseling and that costs will be taken care of by the state. It's nice that they're there. But it doesn't take long before I'm irritated by their presence, before I want to scream at them as they follow me to the restroom. They *follow me* to the *restroom.*

I have a class that morning, and then in the afternoon I'll see the students I was with when the shooting happened. Will they even be there? I have little memory of the morning class; a friend who works as a student advisor and some other man I didn't know and whose role I don't remember, stay with me in class as backup. We talk about what happened, just the facts. But the students want to know why he did it, and I have nothing to tell them. (Later the newspaper will report that when the police asked him this question, he said he'd been having a bad week.) I have wept in front of students only twice: on September 11, and that day. They send me the sweetest emails later, and throughout the week. I feel like I am living only for them.

I tell my students, *The conclusion is your "so what?" Why should we care? What is at stake if we act, or don't act, as you've argued?* A conclusion is another kind of door, I realize. The introduction welcomes you in; the conclusion ushers you out, confident that you have learned something and will walk through the world with fresh eyes.

Why should we care? What is at stake?

Email to my students, April 12, 2013, the night of the shooting:

Dear, dear class,

I feel the need to check in with you and make sure you are all okay. You all scattered so quickly. I am thinking of you and holding you all in my heart.

My computer is at school, so if you email me and I don't respond quickly, that is why. I'm writing this from the Tech library.

Please take care of yourselves.

Megan

THIS EMAIL is more than ten years old. I sound so calm. I didn't know then who was hurt and how badly, what it would be like to go back to school, how completely riven I would be from then on. How little I knew about what life would be like! I don't know if I am writing to them or to myself.

I think about that a lot, now. Whenever people say "This isn't who we are" or "Let it go" or "We will prevail," I think they are talking to themselves. They're not talking to me.

Post-Shooting Lesson Plans

Wednesday, April 17, 2013

What to say . . .

- Ask Ss how they are doing
- What questions they want to ask: fact based
- Then share emotional states
- Let them know that they do not have to talk to media—they can always say no if they are approached
- Let them know about counselors throughout the school
- Victims assistance funds through the state: will pay co-pays for counseling, meds, travel to support groups, etc. If you THINK you might need the help later, even if you are OK now, you should consider signing up with them. If you were here on Friday during the shooting, you are considered a crime victim.
- Grades and the rest of the semester: if they want to take the grades they had and be done, we will accommodate that
- If people feel like they cannot come back to class, that is fine—you can have the grade you have now
- If they want to keep going, we will keep going with them
- If they want to keep going and <u>then later</u> decide to take the grades they have as of now, we will do that
- Most recent papers: I don't feel like I can grade them. So to honor the work that you did, you will all get an A for effort, if you submitted a paper. If you want me to **really** grade it, I will, but if you are OK with just getting a 90, you will.
- Events at main campus at 10 (let them leave early if they want to attend) and at the mall at 3.
- Reminders: Office hours next week: April 23 I have to attend a dept. meeting in Dublin at 11, so will need to go over there and shorten OH. April 22 I will have to run out at 10 to help someone else get to an appt. but will be back within the hour.

South Africa: The Beginning

What did I know about the fifty-five (give or take) countries of Africa? I carried within me one deep personal thread of one small part of it, and it had changed and colored everything.

—Alexandra Fuller, *Leaving Before the Rains Come*

SINCE THE SHOOTING, I find myself breaking words apart, making use of my high school Latin to extract the core components. If I can get to the heart of what they really mean, I will find something true and illuminating. The world I live in doesn't make sense any more, and words are the only thing that I feel like I can depend on: "She had always wanted words, she loved them; grew up on them. Words gave her clarity, brought reason, shape."

This is the best and worst of my character, I think—the impulse/compulsion to excavate everything, to leave no path unexplored as I try to figure this out. Always I look to words for a solution, a mirror, a code, a map. If I stop trying, it means they have failed me.

ALL OF THIS BOOK has been difficult to write, sometimes impossible, but the parts about South Africa are the hardest. I spin my mental wheels endlessly, reading other people's work, annotating, staring out the window, and absently playing with one of the pendants I often wear: a silver Southern Cross or a golden Africa. The stakes feel so high. Who am I to write about South Africa? My race, my nationality ought to exclude me from voicing any opinions or laying any claim to knowledge about the country and the people. I reread Archbishop Trevor Huddleston's memoir *Naught for Your Comfort*, about serving in Sophiatown township outside Johannesburg in the 1940s and '50s: "Without sentimentality or foolish regrets it is most necessary to try to evaluate one's feelings, to try to discover and to relate that strange but deeply real truth which so many have experienced—the witchery of Africa: the way it lays its hold upon your heart and will not let you go."

I don't know if it's his clerical cloak or his sex or his race that give him such confidence. Or maybe he just believes South Africa can hold his story, along with so many others.

2007

When I applied for a Fulbright-Hays summer fellowship, there were only a few country options, among them Brazil and South Africa. I was not particularly interested in Brazil. I was put off by its location in South *America*, too proximate. Even then, I was exoticizing Africa. The acceptance came in February, and our group of about twenty high school and college educators would depart in July. Ostensibly, the purpose of the seminar in South Africa was to learn about how educational institutions were tackling the inequities left by decades of apartheid. Reality was very different.

We had four or five days of orientation in Washington, DC before flying to Johannesburg. A State Department official described culture shock and the stages of adjustment, and she said, "Africa will change some of you forever. You will never be able to truly leave." I inwardly rolled my eyes at such a ridiculous comment. Hadn't she heard all the stereotypes about Westerners who fall in love with Mother Africa?

I knew nothing.

ON NELSON MANDELA'S BIRTHDAY, July 18, 2007, our Fulbright group was divided into small cohorts and sent to various townships—Mamelodi, Soshanguve, Laudium—around the capital city, Pretoria, so that we could visit schools and observe classes. I was sent to Atteridgeville, to David Hellen (D. H.) Peta Secondary School. Atteridgeville was built in 1939, when the Black residents of the Marabastad neighborhood in Pretoria were moved. Indian and Coloured (meaning multi-racial, in South Africa's terms) residents were sent to other areas. In the 1980s, there were frequent demonstrations, some violent, against the apartheid regime. Fifteen-year-old Emma Sathekge, a D. H. Peta student, died in 1984 after being run over by a police vehicle, the first victim of police violence. The *New York Times* reported that year: "A police spokesman in Pretoria said the police fired tear gas after pupils boycotting classes at D. H. Peta High School began throwing stones at them. The police spokesman said a number of children were taken to the hospital, one died and the cause of death was still being investigated."

The schools were closed for much of the year.

The *Times* article about Emma Sathekge concludes, "Miss Sathekge's mother, Sarah, said she was called by another female student and told that her daughter had been taken to the hospital. She said she was told at the hospital that Emma had been X-rayed twice. 'Then they told me that my child was dead,' Mrs. Sathekge said."

I DON'T KNOW what I expected from my first visit to a township, but if I imagined a disaster scene, Atteridgeville wasn't it. The streets were calm, with men walking to work, queuing for an overcrowded taxi, or middle-aged women selling food on a corner. I had my first *vetkoek* from a street vendor, and burned my mouth on the piping minced curry inside a fluffy doughnut-like round. Pyramid-shaped sandwich boards on the sidewalk advertised herbal cures for AIDS, alongside coffin makers and cemetery plots.

At D. H. Peta, kids in neat maroon uniforms piped with gold (my own high school colors) clustered in the doorways and giggled at me and the two other American teachers in my small group. We observed classes where three teenagers crowded together at one desk and shared a single notebook or pen. I was given a desk to myself, and toted a spotless, brand-new spiral notebook that I'd brought to South Africa just for this seminar, as well as a clutch of gaily colored gel pens.

I couldn't hear the teacher, and for a while I wasn't sure why, because none of the kids were talking over him. Then I looked up and saw that the classroom walls were not built all the way to the ceiling, that there was a gap of about eight inches between the roof and the top of the wall, and the noise was coming from the classrooms on either side of us. Pigeons fluttered, cooed, and roosted atop the wall. Streaks of white bird shit dripped down the cinder blocks.

A teacher from D. H. Peta named Peggy Sekhu was assigned to shepherd the two other American teachers and me around Atteridgeville proper and into the informal settlement; she corralled two students to accompany us. The students lived in the informal settlement, which technically is still part of Atteridgeville, but on the outskirts of the township, as the township is on the outskirts of the city. "Informal settlement" is an academic-sounding term for a community that is illegally built on municipal land. Most people just referred to it as "the shacks." In the shacks, houses are constructed of whatever materials are available. Roofs made of sheets of tin, secured with concrete blocks or bricks. Walls might be planks of wood, or bricks, or combinations. The streets were unmarked, dirt, sometimes muddy. I couldn't imagine how people found their way. There were goats. Children playing. Mounds of trash. In the distance a row of pit toilets, with flimsy walls for privacy. All over the country, children fall into latrines and drown with hideous regularity.

Peggy took us to the home of a *sangoma*, or traditional healer, in the settlement. She took us to Leratong Hospice, a facility for AIDS patients run by an Irish priest. (In later years, after our visit, he was badly beaten and sent back to Ireland; the hospice remains supported by Irish parishioners and donations from abroad.) It was spotless and peaceful. The sisters, or nurses, dressed in bright white *doeks* (headdresses) and gray pinafores, told us regretfully that none of the patients wanted to speak at the moment, and I was stunned at the idea that this might be anomalous, that someone might actually want to talk to a foreign white visitor, popping in and out for an afternoon.

FOR THE NEXT SEVERAL WEEKS, we visited universities, FET (Further Education and Training) colleges, primary schools, and high schools all over the country. The pace was exhausting, and as in any group field trip, personalities melded, clashed, flared. I tried to write. I tried to keep my eyes open.

CLOSE TO THE END of the seminar, in early August, we returned to Gauteng Province and visited the Apartheid Museum. The museum, which opened in 2001 (seven years after the first democratic elections), chronicles the insidious laws leading up to total racial segregation and the stranglehold that the national government attempted to maintain.

It begins with the mines: the discovery of gold and diamonds that catapults South Africa from a backwater colony of the British Empire to something worth keeping. Black miners are paid less than Whites, exploited from the beginning. The Group Areas Act, the Immorality Act, the Bantu Education Act: the totality of these laws creates a country where ten percent of the population controls virtually all the capital. The museum narrates the long and violent years of struggle: Nelson Mandela, in prison for twenty-seven years; Archbishop Desmond Tutu, who facilitated the Truth and Reconciliation Commission hearings; the story of Indian resistance fighter Ahmed Kathrada, who was incarcerated with Mandela; the Black Sash human rights organization; the

Women's March in Pretoria in 1957 (*You strike a woman, you strike a rock*); Afrikaner president F. W. de Klerk unbanning various political parties to the shock of the white government. The museum ends with aerial photographs of people queuing to vote in 1994, during the first free election in the country's history.

The word "museum" comes from the Greek *mouseion*, a place for the Muses, minor goddesses of the arts. There were nine of them, the daughters of Zeus and Mnemosyne, the goddess of memory. This is apt, I think, that the word for a repository of the past is, like its namesakes, a descendant of remembrance. A museum shows what we believe is beautiful, dreadful, worth memorializing. That South Africa con-structed such a monument to its recent past, so soon after the transition to democracy, shocked me. Its existence was urgent. And there is nothing sloppy or haphazard about it; it is thor-ough, accurate, and emotionally intense. The entire month I had sensed a courage in South Africa that was lacking in the United States. The Apartheid Museum is a monument to the recent past and to the leaders who risked everything for lib-eration. The people decided that it was worth remembering. Amnesia was not a prerequisite for progress.

WE VISITED SEVEN of the nine provinces in that one month, missing only the Northern Cape and the Free State. There was never enough time to be with other teachers and kids; the pace was exhausting. Maybe, then, what happened the last night was to be expected.

Journal entry: Half past five, August 12, 2007
The light is like golden silk over the highveld. I want to swallow this country.

THE SOUTHERN CROSS is the most recognizable constellation of the Southern Hemisphere; on August 12, 2007, our last night in South Africa, at a celebratory *braai* at the Cradle of Humankind where the oldest human fossils have been unearthed, we were fed and feted yet again, and as the light faded and people began to drum, I crept off into the bush and quietly cried in the dark, those stars silent and aloof above me. Crying with what? Shame that I hadn't the right to weep, or to love the country? An inchoate knowledge that I was never going to be the same, would never be able to look away? It was one of those nights where I felt I had no skin, as though my soul was bleeding out of me. I could not stop crying. I sat in the dirt with my knees bunched up to my forehead, shuddering.

A group of men were cleaning up the tables and plates from our supper. I could see their figures in the shadows, carrying fold-up chairs along a path back to a waiting truck. I tried to be quiet, but they heard me, and quieted, listening.

"Someone is upset," I heard one man whisper, and the brush parted, and he sat down next to me, saying nothing.

The In-Between

I came home to Virginia riven and unsteady. Something had been sundered. I wrote about South Africa in my journal constantly, but never publicly, never for anyone's eyes but my own. I was ashamed of how consumed I was, thinking that it confirmed I was every laughable stereotype of an American in thrall to South Africa. I was on a flight to Boston once with a group of students coming home from a mission trip in Malawi, all of them sporting identical T-shirts and elephant-hair bracelets, laughing and joking about the trip. None of them looked like they were filled with shattered glass. I bent my head over my journal and forced back tears. *What's wrong with me?*

2012

I looked for more opportunities to go back to Africa. In 2010 and again in 2012, I participated in a faculty exchange with a technical university in Sunyani, Ghana. It was joy.

But I wrote in my journal just before leaving for Ghana the second time: *I don't want to be married anymore.*

I couldn't say why, other than that I was unhappy, which seemed like a lame reason to end a marriage. No, that isn't right: I could have said why. But it was too scary, and I was too ashamed. My husband drank. I withdrew. He drank more. I withdrew further. It's a singular story and a universal one, I suppose. He knew Africa had taken root in me, and did not want to risk himself.

I had wanted to go back to D. H. Peta since that first visit in 2007, so I arranged to fly from Accra to Johannesburg after the Ghana exchange ended. My friend Annemarie, a psychology professor at one of the other community colleges and another participant on the exchange, agreed to come with me. I knew I wouldn't be able to drive there (left side, aggressive traffic) and asked the proprietor of the guest house where I'd booked our stay for a driver recommendation. She connected me with a man named Phillip, who would pick up Annemarie and me at the airport and drive us wherever we needed to go.

I didn't know this until later, but Phillip had asked his friend Johan to come with him to fetch us. *I have to get two American girls at the airport,* he said. *Want to come?* Johan was working as a tour guide at the time, after recovering from a brain tumor that had cost him his career as a commercial pilot. *Sure,* Johan replied.

He tells me later that I looked too young to be a professor, but that I strode through the arrivals hall in O. R. Tambo International Airport, all business, hand outstretched, smiling, joyful. I loved him from almost the first moment I set eyes on him.

FOR THE FIRST TIME, I tentatively unloaded all the fear and shame and uncertainty I had carried since coming to South Africa the first time. *I think I love your country. I want to understand everything about it. Everything here is real and honest. Am I normal? Is this okay?*

Yes, he said. *Yes.*

THE NIGHT BEFORE WE FLEW HOME, at dinner, I gave him a copy of *Wind, Sand, and Stars.* It's written by Antoine de Saint-Exupéry, better known for *The Little Prince,* but this one is about his flying days over the Sahara. I thought there had to be a sign there, that I was carrying around a memoir by a pilot in Africa and had just met . . . a pilot in Africa.

The next morning, before Phillip drove Annemarie and me back to the airport, Johan handed me a copy of J. M. Coetzee's novel *Disgrace*. Inside, he'd written:

Dear Megan

You and the lead character of this book have a profession in common, but not much else. Maybe it will help explain why some of us have become so emotionally detached in SA.

You wear your heart on your sleeve. And what a beautiful heart it is. One that truly feels. To be willing to risk such agony on behalf of others takes enormous strength and courage. If we were all willing to do that, the world would be near-perfect.

Thank you for loving my country. Thank you for your sincere and immediate empathy for its wide-eyed children.

Johan

THE DAY AFTER I GOT HOME to Virginia, Tom asked me, "Did you meet someone?"

I sank down to sit on the kitchen floor, sick with guilt. "Yes, I think so."

Tom seemed unbothered. I asked him, "Have you ever felt a connection with someone else?" After all, we regularly spent months apart, when he was at his field research site. I knew the close proximity he worked in with just a few others, the extreme remoteness of the area.

"Yeah," he said. "There are connections."

THE SUMMER OF 2012 was wretched, the worst months of my life up to that point. I yearned to go back to South Africa. I did not know what to do about my feelings for Johan. We had continued to email and when I felt we crossed a line into an emotional affair (a phrase I learned from scouring infidelity forums), I told him we could never speak again and I begged Tom's forgiveness for letting my feelings get out of hand. *I love you*, I wailed, *I am so sorry I never meant for this to happen please forgive me I'll never talk to him again.*

Tom listened and then said, "You don't need to stop talking to him."

I stopped crying.

"Do you hear me saying I have feelings for someone else?"

"Yeah," Tom said. "I hear you."

I thought that proved how wise and rational he was, that I was the unstable lunatic wife, that he knew these things happened and it would all be right in the end. Oh, you stupid, stupid girl.

I was also sure that South Africa wasn't done with me, that there were things I needed to understand about myself and my own country that I could only learn there. When Tom and I had first gotten together, I had given up a Peace Corps posting to be with him. A few years into our marriage we had applied for yearlong Fulbright fellowships together, and when I received one and he didn't, he refused to come with me. I felt like time was slipping away and that if I didn't seize the opportunity now, I never would. I was starting to realize how short life really was and how urgently I had to live it, a realization that would hit me even harder after the shooting. But at the time, I could not see how to do it.

IT WAS JUNE when I felt the first hint of something amiss. In the shower, washing between my legs, I felt a slight catch, a momentary roughness. After emerging, I squatted over a mirror to see better. On the surface of my flesh, I saw some discoloration, a pale smudge, and when I touched it I recognized the strange texture. I thought for a minute, then decided to see if it didn't go away on its own.

It didn't go away on its own. I looked the symptoms up online again, and soon I'd narrowed it down to either genital warts or cancer. Both seemed highly suspect. I'd been married for twelve years and only had three partners in my entire life, so an STD seemed really improbable, and that kind of cancer was quite rare. Some other explanation had to exist.

My doctor was kind. He listened to me describe the rough patches, and instructed me to disrobe when he left the room. Scooching down to the end of the table, I opened my legs and fit my feet into the stirrups. The ceiling was decorated with a poster of a kitten clinging to a tree branch (*Hang in there!*) and I wondered what posters are on the ceiling in exam rooms where men get their prostates checked.

I heard the words and started to cry. *Genital warts*, he said. I saw the looks he and the nurse exchanged but all I could do was cry.

They gave me a prescription for Aldara cream. I found out later that it's used to treat skin cancer.

When I got home, I was nearly hysterical. I had sobbed in the car and my cheeks were streaked with wet mascara, my eyes almost swollen shut. Tom hugged me and told me he was so sorry. *I was promiscuous in college*, he said. *It's my fault.*

The treatment hurt.

Later in the summer, when I was tearfully venting about the pain, Tom scolded me and said I wasn't handling my diagnosis very well.

In October, I shared the state of my marriage with some friends. One leaned across the table and told me that she thought Tom was having an affair. *Really?* I asked. *Yes*, she told me. *You got an STD twelve years into your marriage and you told him you were in love with someone else and he said that's fine? You have to ask him.*

Huh, I thought.

That night I said, *I need to ask you something. I'll only ask once, and I will believe whatever you tell me. Have you ever strayed?*

All the air left the room.

FRAGMENTS of the last two years snapped together with flinty, cold edges. When I had received an email from an unfamiliar account, telling me *there's something you need to know about Tom but he can't know I told you.* When he told me he was at a conference, he was really with her, getting "closure." When he told me that I'd gotten genital warts because he was promiscuous in college twenty years ago, he hadn't mentioned he'd been fucking someone else.

I threw clothes into an overnight bag and left the house. We never lived together again.

I went to the doctor again the day after, whispering furtively to the appointment counselor behind the front desk. *I need a full sexually transmitted disease workup.* I wonder now how many times they've heard that same story, seen a broken-eyed woman at the appointment desk muttering under her breath because she can hardly bring herself to name what's truly happening.

Again, I lay on my back on the table staring up at the strange pockmarked industrial ceiling. I bared my arm to the elbow in the phlebotomy corridor where another nurse in lollipop scrubs tied a piece of lime-green sticky tape around my elbow to make the vein pop. The needle slid in. The kind-eyed nurse took two vials. I could not stop crying.

I told Johan what had happened. He sent me an email:

Dearest Megan,

> *I am so sorry this was done to you. I am shell-shocked, angry and concerned. I don't know how you need to handle this. I just know that you can. You have the spirit of a lion and you will not be broken.*

> *I am thinking of you every second. Thank you for putting confidence in me.*

> *You are a remarkable woman. You may not make any of this your fault. None of it is. I cannot imagine how anyone who loves you and who is loved by you, would ever dare jeopardise that love.*

> *What can be more precious.*

> *Yours always, Johan*

Sanctuary

Three years I had there. Alone. At peace.
Often I awoke as the light began to cease.
The house breathed and shook like a lover
as I took for myself time needed to recover.
        —Spencer Reece, "Then"

I MOVE INTO A NEW HOUSE a month after leaving Tom. It be-
longs to some friends; they remodeled it and lived here before
buying a bigger home, and now they rent this one out. The
elderly woman who lives across the street once lived in this
house, too, before it had indoor plumbing. It is tiny—about
as tiny as a house can be without actually being a tiny house.
Four rooms: a front room; kitchen; two bedrooms; a tiny bath
with a window in the shower, looking out on the backyard.
The house is painted green, with white trim and reddish shingles. It matches the green hills and what I come to call "the
paddock" just beyond, an overgrown pasture. There is a little
stream in the front yard, and after heavy rain or snowmelt,
water rushes through it, another instrument in the house's
song.

    The kitchen window looks out onto a small outcropping,

where the owners have planted flowers, but native vines are snaking through the crevices. Sometimes, when I'm washing the dishes, I watch a little groundhog family scamper around, and brazen deer come nearly to the window nibbling on the overgrown grass. I stake solar lights in the cracks between the stones, and in winter, they gleam faintly through the snow like fireflies. It's like I live in the Shire.

Best of all, though, is the yoga hut. The backyard juts up at a steep angle, making mowing a real chore, but at the high point of the yard is an outbuilding with a porch and fairy lights strung along the roofline. Inside, the back wall is painted cobalt blue, and there is a laminate wood floor and slanted windows on either side. I take my yoga mat and blocks and an extra CD player to the hut, and when I don't feel like driving to the studio, I go up there and practice. I can stand in tree pose and look out over the roof of the tiny house just below and the forested ridgeline on the other side of the road.

In the morning, before school, I get up in the dark and take my dog, Daisy, out for a walk. There are rarely cars on the road this early, though we frequently meet a man riding his bike to work. His headlamp and blinker flash crimson and white out of the dark, and as he zooms past us, Daisy lunges and yelps at him. We listen to the birds at daybreak, we surprise a fawn hidden in the tall grass; one day Daisy stops to pee on a black racer, which slithers away in disgust. Another morning, three deer leap in front of us, and beyond them, a black bear lopes across the road.

Every day when I come home, the house is just as I left it. My Daisy ambles to the door, her feathered tail swishing, and she leans on me as I set my bookbag down. At night, she keeps me company in the front room before coming to bed for the night. With her and Olivia, my longhaired tortoiseshell cat, the night seems so friendly, a place I can rest. Most people think that nights in the country are quiet, but in summer, the crickets and peepers launch a clamorous symphony. As long as Daisy is sleeping, I know nothing is wrong. It seems so simple and so right to put my trust in her. Sometimes I even forget to close the kitchen door, which leads onto the screened porch, and I don't see my mistake until morning. Nothing happens.

It is clear to me from the first week of living in the house that I will never go back to Tom. Although our separation is, initially, on paper, only for six months, I know that this is the end. From the first night I spend in the tiny green house, I sleep in a way that I cannot recall having slept in a long, long time. There are so many entries in my journals from the past few years, written at two or three in the morning, that start something like this: "He's passed out drunk again," or "He tried to walk out the door with the car keys, and I had to stop him." I had not realized how forcefully I was holding my breath, living with him, until I came to the tiny green house and exhaled. I hadn't realized how tentatively I had been moving through that life until I left it.

During my first spring in the new house, a friend invites me to an information session about the local women's shelter. The program director begins with a litany of facts about domestic violence in our area. She shows slides of the safe house, without revealing its exterior. It's comfortable and homey, with a big kitchen and bunk beds, plenty of books and toys, laundry facilities. From the outside, you would never know its true purpose. She explains the protocol for how they respond to calls for help.

"The first thing we ask when a woman calls us is 'Are you safe?'" she says. "Sometimes women say yes. Sometimes they say 'Well, I don't know, he's drunk and he's got a gun and he's just gone out for more beer.' Our first priority is to establish whether the caller and children, if there are children, are safe."

Are you safe?

Sitting in the back of the conference room with my cup of water and plate of snacks, I wonder how I would have answered that question, had someone ever asked me. What would I have said on all the nights when Tom was up late drinking and finally stumbled into bed, while I waited until two or three in the morning, reading, writing, forcing myself to stay awake so that if some emergency happened, I'd be able to deal with it? What would I have said the night that he got so angry he yanked the smoke alarm off the ceiling and hurled it into the yard, leaving only wire tentacles in its place? What would I have said the night that he was so drunk that he tore a door out of the wall by its hinges, believing the house was falling down? Why didn't I ask *myself* whether I was safe?

In previous journal entries, I had written *I'm so unhappy*. I could name my misery only as happiness/unhappiness, rather than a state of danger. Unhappiness was easier to dismiss. I recognized it, but wrote, as if in conversation with myself, *Who's happy? Is anyone? Who are you to ask to be happy?* How dif-

ferent my answer would have been if I had asked, *Are you safe?*
I like to think that I would never have told myself, *Who are you
to want to feel safe?* I hope that I would have seen that as the ne-
cessity it was, not a luxury I had no right to demand.

Some months later, at a Starbucks, I meet one of the
other faculty members who was teaching on the afternoon of
the shooting. The shooter came straight to his classroom and
opened fire, while the students scrambled under desks. This
professor tells me that he's got a concealed-carry permit and
if only he'd been able to have his gun that day, he could have
stopped the shooter. He says that he hates being alone now,
that the only time he feels safe is when there are crowds of
other people around.

I know that everyone processes trauma differently, but I
hate being around other people. There is nowhere I'd rather
be than alone in my little house. There, no one will throw or
break things. There are no guns, so no one will shoot me.
Even though my house is just a bit outside the town limits, it
feels like it's far out in the country, though not far enough for
me. Sometimes I daydream about a house in the woods for
just myself and my animals, an enchanted cottage deep in
the forest where I don't have to see or encounter another person. People are the problem. Not just people: men. Men and
guns.

Protection, it turns out, is the number one reason why
people own guns. From one another, from strangers bent on
harm, from a government determined to confiscate them—
for some, a gun assumes a talismanic power to repel any
forces of evil, human or otherwise. Research from Harvard's

School of Public Health, though, reveals over and over again that the presence of a gun in the home dramatically increases the risks of homicide and suicide alike.

When Johan and I first began to correspond over email, I introduced him to one of my favorite writers, Zimbabwean memoirist Alexandra Fuller. Like him, she is a white African, and like him, she finds both intolerable burden and extraordinary grace in this complicated identity. Fuller is one of two surviving daughters; her parents lost three other children to illness and accident, yet insisted that Zimbabwe was home. "In the West," writes Fuller, "it was believed that attitude and ambition saved you. In Africa, we had learned no one was immune to capricious tragedy." Her upbringing is scarred not only by war, but by quotidian perils like cobras in the pantry. Safety was never an expectation in her life; how could she grow up with three dead siblings and believe that the world was a benevolent place?

WHEN JOHAN AND I returned from South Africa in 2016, we moved back into my tiny house for a few months, but it was clear that the stay had to be temporary. But I was so reluctant to leave it. It was the refuge I had fled to from an unsafe marriage, where I was able to sweep up the fragments of myself and rearrange them into something that vaguely resembled the person I had been before my divorce and before the shooting. Though I couldn't quite articulate it at the time, I had given the house the power of a binding spell: outside it, I would fall apart again. But the house began to give me increasingly stern orders to leave; it was only, ever, for me and my animals. It's like Hogwarts Castle's Room of Requirement: it appears just when you need it and it is precisely what you need; it isn't made to live in permanently.

THE SAFETY that the house had given me was not particular to the house itself; I could leave it, and retain the memory of that peace. It wasn't to be found only in the house. It was in me.

South Africa: The Middle

2014

In my atlas, Africa takes up nearly eight pages, the corners and center divided up and enlarged so that I can see every river, every careless, haphazard boundary drawn by white people decades ago. European colonial powers mapped national boundaries by trade routes that would benefit their scramble for Africa, ignoring the natural features of the land, the languages and cultures as though there were no people at all, just a featureless, uninhabited mass for the stealing. Even the names change: Upper Volta becomes Burkina Faso; Northern Rhodesia, Zambia; South West Africa, Namibia. Geographical orientations make way for the names of the people. The fluidity of place-names and boundaries marked by people with mercenary stakes in the land seems to illuminate the ways that people from outside try to quantify the unquantifiable, to attach their own meaning to places that exist independent of their paradigms (as I do). I spent drowsy evenings poring over the Africa pages. I felt like I was mapping the life I wanted to have. It was not just Johan drawing me back to southern Africa, though I knew that my love flowering for him needed time to root in that arid soil and be fed with the December rain. I wore my pendant in the shape of the Southern Cross that I fidgeted with throughout the day, as though I could make it point me in that direction, south, home.

Migratio, Latin. "Removal, change of abode, migration." Because money, of course, was an issue, I turned to the Fulbright program, the one that first brought me to South Africa. Not just a summer for me, this time—I was going to go for the year. The Fulbright's catalogue page for South Africa noted that the program makes it a point to place people across the country, not just in Johannesburg and Cape Town.

Fine with me. I had been to both cities, but each of them is full of tourists, diplomats, and other international types. I wanted as few encounters with other Americans as possible. Which is how I found myself on the web page for the University of the Free State (UFS), in Bloemfontein. The City of Roses, judicial capital of South Africa where the Supreme Court of Appeals convenes, Bloem is in the center of the country and the capital of the Free State province. The Free State isn't home to the kinds of attractions that generally draw scholars or tourists; it was one of only two provinces that we hadn't visited on the Fulbright seminar.

In Bloemfontein, there is a museum to Afrikaans literature; a museum of the Boer War, where I learn the words *bittereinder* and *hensopper*, words no longer in common use but still weighty with what I come to call the bleeding, fatal pride of the Afrikaner people; a contemporary art museum in the Dutch-colonial style; a nature reserve on Naval Hill with a gigantic statue of Nelson Mandela and resident giraffes and zebras; and a botanical garden at the upper ridge of the city that is a cool, leafy oasis from the heat.

So I chose the Free State, and the university there. I connected with the English department head and secured a formal invitation to teach and do research. I talked with Dr. Pumla Godobo-Madikizela, the director of the Institute for Trauma, Reconciliation, and Forgiveness Studies at UFS, who served on the Truth and Reconciliation Commission (TRC), about what the United States can learn about public witness, accountability, restitution. I secured enthusiastic letters of reference and crafted a stellar proposal to use the lessons of the TRC to inform a system of restorative justice and truth-telling about the impact of school gun violence in the United States. I was so proud of my work. I felt sure that it would stand out from the crowd. I submitted it in the summer of 2014.

In November, I received a terse email that my proposal hadn't passed into the second stage of review. Reading it was a punch to my heart. I couldn't understand it. I had a letter of support from someone who was on the TRC; I was writing about something urgent, in which I had a profound stake. How was this not enough? The shock was compounded by the statement that no comments or feedback would be given; there was no one to ask why, or what I could have done better. *What a ridiculous practice*, I thought, completely antithetical to the learning process. It occurred to me much later that because of a rider attached to a 1996 appropriations bill funding the Centers for Disease Control, the federal government was prevented from using its own money to fund gun violence research. The State Department is a federal division. I consoled myself with the slim possibility that maybe they wanted to support my proposal, but couldn't.

THE NEXT MORNING I decided, *Fuck you. I'm going anyway.*

I UPROOTED EVERYTHING: I obtained permission to take a year's sabbatical. I talked with my bank about transferring funds overseas. I secured a visa. I registered with the State Department's website for Americans abroad. I alerted my health insurance company. I sublet the tiny green house and moved all my possessions into a storage unit. I taught four classes the summer before I departed, to build up my savings as much as possible. I secured housing on campus. I booked a flight. I gave my sister a key to my safe deposit box. I compiled a document for my parents with all my account numbers and passwords, and a short directive about what to do with my remains if I was killed while I was gone, complete with the hymns I want them to sing.

PLANNING FOR MY OWN DEATH is something I have become more familiar with.

I ARRIVED IN BLOEM in August 2015. I lived in an on-campus residence for international graduate students and researchers. It was as comfortable as any hotel. I shared a kitchen with the others on my floor: scholars from Zimbabwe, eSwatini, Italy, Nigeria, Ethiopia, Australia, Canada.

I explored the campus daily on foot. I rolled the strange building names around in my head before attempting them with my tongue: Wag n' Bietjie, or "wait-a-bit"; Tswelopele, the name of a local municipality; Welwitschia, a gigantic desert succulent; Soetdoring, or "sweet thorn." My office was in the pragmatically named Flippie Groenewoud Building, across from Sielkunde, Psychology. Johan told me that *sielkunde* literally means "soul care."

My residence was at the far end of campus, near the athletic fields. In time, I plotted an evening walk that took me across dry fields where yellow mongooses popped their cheeky heads up out of the pale golden grass. Past the rugby pitch, where in February a riot erupted after Black students protesting the outsourcing of low-level positions were attacked by white rugby players. Past the soccer fields, the clubhouses, the tennis courts. I walked every evening, when the day's heat had dissipated into a dry, comfortable warmth. Each step felt like a small claim on this land that I loved so much but knew would never be mine. The province's sparse beauty—its long, exposed blond and wheat and rust and ocher fields, its occasional pensive secretary bird, its sudden *kopje*—made me want to get out of the car or bus and just walk, walk for miles and ever. It was nothing to imagine a cheetah streaking across the veldt, or placidly lying in wait concealed by the high grass.

I never once had to run from a shooter.

BEFORE COMING TO BLOEMFONTEIN, I had printed out dozens of scholarly articles on the Truth and Reconciliation Commission, hoping, as I had stated in my defunct Fulbright application, to think of what it might look like to bear public witness about school gun violence in the United States. The purpose of the TRC had been to publicly speak the truth about human rights violence committed during apartheid. Families of the murdered and disappeared could finally get answers; perpetrators were offered amnesty for confessing what they had done. The South African Broadcasting Company had broadcast the testimonies on television for two months in 1996. The material impact of the TRC is debatable, and in my year in Bloem I heard plenty of critique that South Africa, and Mandela, had paid too much attention to reconciliation and not enough to recompense. I see this and acknowledge it. Years of control by the African National Congress, Mandela's party, hasn't lifted the majority of Black South Africans out of poverty, nor has it made up for generations of financial deprivation and educational inequity. From my American perspective, though, the mere fact of publicly acknowledging wrongdoing seemed momentous. American culture is all about forward momentum; if we pause to look at the past it's just that, a pause, not a sustained examination of where we've come from and how we might learn from history.

An important narrative of the TRC is *Country of My Skull: Guilt, Sorrow, and the Limits of Forgiveness in the New South Africa*, by Afrikaner poet and journalist Antjie Krog. There are three kinds of memory loss, writes Krog. "The first is voluntary—you change your memory because you are under threat, because you cannot bear to live with the reality. The second is involuntary—something so traumatic that it rips a hole in your memory, and you cannot remember the incident or what happened just before and after it. But there is also a third kind of memory loss and that occurs when you testify in public. Because of these narratives, people can no longer indulge in their separate dynasties of denial."

I READ that last sentence, now—that you cannot indulge in a dynasty of denial—and dismiss it out of hand. Krog is writing about the TRC and the public broadcast testimonies of murder, torture, and disappearance wrought by the apartheid struggle. In South Africa, perhaps, no one can say *we didn't know*. The country made sure that everyone would know. "A community should not wipe out a part of its past, because it leaves a vacuum that will be filled by lies and contradictory, confusing accounts of what happened," she said.

If we in the U.S. heard testimonies from the teachers and students who'd been injured and traumatized in school shootings, from the families of the dead, would Americans be moved enough to act? Cowardly, pathetic, craven, oh, here in the United States we will take great care that people do not know. We wrap words like *liberty* and *freedom* around the bodies of the dead and clean up the blood and make sure that you never have to look at them again.

Too, I know now how Americans ask for amnesty after every mass shooting. That for me is the worst, most unbearable part of life after the shooting: knowing that there is no amount of suffering, death, testimony, or witnessing that will stop firearm violence. There is no evidence reliable enough, objective enough, to convince Republican congresspeople and state lawmakers that their beliefs about guns and freedom are lethal. They will always move the goalposts, build a straw man, hurl an ad populum fallacy. There are no 911 calls from children staring at their teacher's corpse graphic enough, tragic enough, pitiable enough, to move the people in power to say *No more*.

In an interview with the *New York Times* in 2020, Dr. Gobodo-Madikizela does not sugarcoat the commission's shortcomings, and acknowledges that the average Black South African's material circumstances didn't improve as a result of the hearings. The TRC's biggest success, she asserts, was "witnessing the possibility that things can be different." I remember this interview when I read Jennifer Carlson's article "From a Society of Survivors to a Survivor Society." Carlson is a professor at the University of Arizona and has written widely about policing, Second Amendment rights, and most recently about gun sellers. In this article, Carlson recounts the interviews she's done with gun violence survivors, and emphasizes that gun trauma is not just an individual despair. It is exacerbated by systems that ignore victims and survivors, and ensure that violence will continue.

All I have ever wanted, since my shooting, is to make sure that this will never happen to anyone ever again. I've failed, on my own, to make that happen. That's a terrible pain to carry. But I can get over that. I can get over the memory of that day, the nightmares, I can live with that. What I can't live with is this culture that allows it to happen and then calls *us* the un-American, crazy, tyrannical ones for wanting to spare others. I can't forgive or reconcile with my own culture.

DR. GOBODO-MADIKIZELA reminds her interviewer that "the language of reconciliation is limited when used in isolation from other critical issues of social justice." Real justice means your culture sees pain, sees the mistakes it has made/continues to make, and tries to stop it. So add gun violence to racism, homo- and transphobia, sexism, erasure of Native people and identity to the list of abuses and neglect that can't be remedied through therapy and self-care.

WRITING ABOUT SOUTH AFRICA feels like theft, an act of occupation. Me, white American, trying to articulate what the country is and what it means to me. The arrogance! I can hardly stand myself. Even though Johan tells me I can, and should, I don't fully believe it. I don't know how any white American can confidently write anything about Africa, regardless of how many years you have spent on the continent, how close your ties are. Sixteen years now since the first time I set foot in South Africa, and I am so different. I don't know if I could have learned here what I learned there—or, perhaps, I could have, but it would have required far greater intentional effort on my part, effort that I didn't even know was required and had no idea how to exert. That is the difference, I think. In South Africa there was no way to escape the accountability for my own whiteness and no way to keep so silent.

"Without sentimentality or foolish regrets it is most necessary to try to evaluate one's feelings," as Archbishop Huddleston wrote about how deeply South Africa can seize some visitors. I would like to think that I see the place as clearly as a foreigner can, without sentimentality: I won't gloss over the violence, the chasmic inequity, the governmental corruption there. All that is real.

This is also real, though: South Africa had leaders with extraordinary vision who were willing to sacrifice their families and their lives for an equitable society, and who were willing to negotiate and lose face among their followers, for the greater good. CODESA, a multi-racial, multi-party coalition, crafted a new Constitution in the mid-nineties. (Reread that: They *wrote a new Constitution*, recognizing that the old one did not serve the country they were trying to build. They didn't behave as though the old one had been written by God.) The preamble reads:

> *We, the people of South Africa,*
> *Recognise the injustices of our past;*
> *Honour those who suffered for justice and freedom in our land;*
> *Respect those who have worked to build and develop our country; and*
> *Believe that South Africa belongs to all who live in it, united in our diversity.*

It goes on to codify the rights to education, language access, and reproductive care.

ALAIN DE BOTTON WRITES, "What we find exotic abroad may be what we hunger for in vain at home." South Africa doesn't claim to be the greatest country in Africa, let alone the history of the world. It's honest about what still needs to be done.

If only the United States could say the same.

By My Own Hand

January 2013

I'VE USED THE PARING KNIFE a thousand times to slice cheese and skin a potato. This time, I hold it and imagine the force I'll need to jam it into my own heart.

My marriage is over. But I'm temporarily back in "our" house taking care of the dogs while Tom is at the same research site where he barreled into his affair. The house feels like a prison I've recently been paroled from and then forced to reoccupy. I am riven with shame and fury. Over the past six weeks, Tom has asked me how much longer he's going to have to be the bad guy, how much longer he will have to eat shit over this.

I lean against the sliding glass door and stare out at the night. The house borders national forest land, and the nights are impenetrably dark. My hands are freezing and damp, as though I've been clutching a glass of ice water on an August afternoon.

There is a gun in Tom's desk. I suspect that it's the 9mm I told him to sell a few years ago.

I've never fired a pistol, only the .22 rifle he taught me to use so that I could kill a rabid skunk if I needed to. Will it be easier than the knife? I don't even know how to load it. Maybe he keeps it loaded.

Claws click across the laminate floor. My dog walks into the kitchen, her copper-feather tail slowly wagging. She leans on my thighs, pressing me against the icy glass. I spread my hands on her warm flanks. I can feel her heart beating. She turns her dear face up to mine with such trust, chestnut brown eyes and a muzzle woven with silver.

Who will care for her if I kill myself? Should I call someone and let them know what I'm about to do so that they'll come and care for the animals? What if I frighten the dogs with my own noise?

This is how much of a failure I am: I'm not good enough to warrant my husband's fidelity, and now I'm not strong enough to use the knife, either.

Somehow, I pick up my phone and call my counselor.

"I'm really scared," I tell her. "I'm afraid I am going to hurt myself."

"Come in right away," she tells me.

The night is inky. As I approach the intersection where I must turn left to cross a four-lane divided highway, I look at the lights of oncoming cars and think about turning sharply instead, straight into them. Maybe that's the way to do it. But no, I think; then I'd hurt someone else, maybe kill them instead of my own pathetic self, and that would be worse than dying. My hands drip sweat onto my lap. I clutch the steering wheel and force myself to wait for an opening in the traffic.

I make it to my counselor's office alive.

"A THOROUGH CRISIS is a death experience; we cannot have the one without the other. This implies that the suicidal crisis, because it is one of the ways of experiencing death, must also be considered necessary to the life of the soul," writes James Hillman, a protégé of Carl Jung and author of *Suicide and the Soul.*

MY SHOOTER was sentenced to thirty-eight years in prison in the summer of 2014. In court, he told the women he'd shot to "stay strong." This, after they had to watch videos of him talking about his desire to kill people, to see their blood and bodies. It seems a singular torture to have to endure the trial of the man who tried to kill you. During the trial, it emerged that he had made at least one suicide attempt. His family swore that they never dreamed he would try to hurt others; he had made suicide attempts before and they only feared he might hurt himself.

I go to new river community college in Christiansburg Virgina. 10 minutes away from Virginia tech. I'm gonna give y'all the details because the news never gets it right. Stevens 320 shotgun. Buck shots and slugs. I'm a bit nervous because I've never really handled a shotgun but a few times with the Christiansburg police. I'm here at school writing this. Wish me luck. An heroing [suicide] is not necessary unless I get fucked out the ass. It's pretty busy.[1]

—Posted April 12, 2013

A *heroing.*

Rachel Kalish and Michael Kimmel assert that among men a completed, or "successful," suicide is perceived more favorably than a nonfatal attempt. There is an element of masculine power in a completed suicide, particularly one involving firearms, which is how most school shooters choose to end their lives.

Anyways, he continued in his post, *this is not a highscores game but actually a lesson (that's why I'm at school).*

I don't know what he meant by "a highscores game." High body count?

---

[1] My shooter took part in the Citizens Police Academy: from the website, "During the academy, participants have a chance to ride along with Christiansburg police officers, visit the firing range and fire the weapons officers carry, and experience a K-9 demonstration. In addition to hands-on activities, participants will take part in classroom instruction, learning how radar works, how DUI stops are made, techniques for defensive tactics and more."

A lesson: I was taught to design my lesson plans with the mnemonic SWBAT: Students Will Be Able To. It's a "begin with the end in mind" approach, focusing on what you want to convey and how to get there.

What did he want us to learn—about him, about what he was capable of?

In Dante's *Inferno*, there is a dim forest for those who have chosen suicide, a haunted tableau of poisonous thorns and groaning trees on whose leaves Harpies feed for eternity: "When departs the fierce soul from the body, by itself thence torn asunder, to the seventh gulf by Minos doom'd, into the wood it falls, no place assign'd, but wheresoever chance hurls it, there sprouting, as a grain of spelt, it rises to a sapling, growing thence a savage plant . . . for what a man takes from himself it is not just he have." The afterlife is its own death sentence, the agony of life unending.

I wonder if, despite the chipper tone of his final online post, my shooter hoped that the police might kill him. Is the "heroing" he imagines by his hand, or another's?

My memory drifts back three years to that afternoon in the doctor's office after Tom confessed his affair, when I was tested for all the sexually transmitted diseases, and the physical horror that I thought would ignite the container of my body. It flared out my fingertips like lightning and left seared burns through my torso. My heart was charred. Dying seemed like the only way to extinguish the fire.

August 2018

Students from Marjory Stoneman Douglas High School in Parkland, Florida, embark on a nationwide tour, picking up on the momentum of the March for Our Lives in Washington a few months earlier. They stop in Blacksburg, of course. Somehow, I volunteer? am voluntold? to be the primary organizer for the event. The kids have a retinue of managers, and their organization is baffling and byzantine. I field daily calls and texts from several people who are clearly not communicating with one another. They bicker over where to hold the town hall and challenge me on the local team's decisions, frustrated that there won't be hordes of college students to attend (forgetting that early August is still summer break), and push back on every choice we make from the ground. I appear on television and in a story on the local NPR station. I have to say the same things I've said a thousand times: that I became an activist because of what happened to me, that I just don't want anyone else to have to live with this. I hate being on television.

I feel my body constrict as the day approaches, a corporeal migraine, as though each vessel is bled dry. I don't sleep well. I am having familiar nightmares again. I keep looking at the calendar as though I can speed up time and imagine August 4, the day after, when this will all be over. So many dates that I wish I could skip.

On the morning of the town hall, we have a private meeting at the Lyric Theater with the Parkland kids and area survivors of gun violence: Colin Goddard, who was shot in the Virginia Tech massacre and now has lead poisoning from the shrapnel left in his body; Andy and Barbara Parker, whose journalist daughter Alison was murdered on local live television in 2015; Alison's fiancé, Chris Hurst, then a delegate to the General Assembly in Richmond; faith leaders; police; other organizers. And me. Later, at the public event, more than four hundred people attend. It's standing room only. Everyone is checked for weapons as they enter. I pace in the aisles, watching the crowd, watching the black-clad members of the Utah Gun Exchange, who have been following the kids around the country in an armored vehicle, as they line up to ask questions. I watch the reporters, watch the kids' security team watching the kids. I don't even listen to the students. I can't tell you anything about what they said that day.

Afterwards, we walk the kids over to the April 16 memorial on the Virginia Tech Drillfield, all the kids whose names you know from television and social media, and I am struck by how young, how heartbreakingly childlike, they seem. They've just been in front of a crowd speaking passionately about the simple wish to live free from violence, and now they bounce on top of each other, toppling ball caps and tugging on the bottles of hand sanitizer and tiny bug-eyed stuffed animals hanging off their backpacks.

But when we approach the memorial, the sober half-circle of thirty-two granite stones with names engraved on each one, they fall silent. I sit with a few who are leaning on each other, their smooth faces suddenly careworn. The reality of their existence is lunacy: traveling around the country on a bus without their parents, staying in hotels, guarded by security (one of the team members tells me that he's horrified by the vile death threats the kids receive daily), stalked by gun nuts everywhere they go. All because they just don't want more people to be murdered in school.

They are so young and so exhausted. I feel as though I am party to their abuse.

I'm wrung out, so tired that I could drop to the grass and sleep for days. Some of the other organizers are giddy with excitement at being in the presence of X González, the iconic person in an army jacket who held heavy minutes of tearful silence at the March for Our Lives in Washington. But all I want is to crawl under my weighted blanket. I don't even go out to dinner with them. I stagger home and get drunk on Pinot Grigio and try to sleep.

In a restorative yoga class a few days after the town hall, I'm trying to lie still and *let the breath ride the length of my body*, as my teacher says. I will it to flow smoothly, but this breath shudders and hesitates, approaching, then fleeing my lungs. How blessed it would be to cease breathing for good, how light I would feel. How unburdened! I am so ashamed of my suffering, and my surety that it is unearned (after all, *I* wasn't shot: why should I be so full of woe?) and that no matter what I do, no matter how far afield I travel, how religiously I take my medicine, how often I practice yoga, how many hours of therapy I engage in (an hour a week for five years? God help me), I am permanently broken, and I will never be okay ever again. I have failed at recovery.

I think of my Tramadol stash in the back of the linen closet. I have entire packets of unopened pills left over from kidney stone surgery in 2016. I know better than to take them all at once. But I recall with sudden longing the hazy pleasure of my night in the hospital when I was mainlining opioids and the delirious relief when the pain finally stopped. If only I could feel that holy oblivion again.

I AM BACK in my counselor's office two days after the kids leave, the breath shuddering out of me. She has ice-white hair, big blue eyes, and an unflappable manner. I tell her that I'm having fantasies about killing myself—I don't think I'm actually going to do it, I know intellectually that this is just temporary, but I can't see myself out of it. *What is wrong with me?*, I wail. *Why am I still so fucked up? I am never going to be all right, am I?* She makes me call my doctor's office right there and instructs me to tell them that it's an emergency, but they can't fit me in for another month. She asks me if I need to be hospitalized. I tell her no. To say yes would be an act of colossal arrogance, I think, putting myself in the same category as the Parkland kids and the women at my school who were actually shot. My students and I got out. It wasn't our blood on the walls. Who am I to need help?

I'm sure I am permanently broken beyond repair and I'm also sure that I do not deserve to be in so much pain.

Summer fades imperceptibly into fall. I go back to school and soon my attention is focused on my own students and the routines of lesson plans and essays. I hide the guilt behind gratitude. Both are real.

March 2019

In a three-week span, two survivors of the Parkland massacre surrender their lives, and then Jeremy Richman, whose daughter Avielle was murdered at Sandy Hook, is found dead in his car, also from suicide.

UNARMED

A suicide may leap free of another's
judging
and fall into
the mystery of the human heart

—Margaret Gibson, "Judge Not"

I LOOK UP THE ETYMOLOGY of the word "lament": *moan, bewail.* Always I try to find clues in the building blocks of a word, a trail of letters and meaning that will lead me out of this darkness.

January 2020

The seventeen-year-old son of an old high school friend ends his life on January 3, 2020. I haven't seen her in years, but we have reconnected through social media. She lives now in an old farmhouse full of sharp angles and shafts of clear northern light that fall through the windows. In the photos she posts online, her two teenaged boys embody the rough beauty of the mountains and the sweetness I remember in their mother. We have been chatting about a visit. Of all the friends of my youth, she is the one I would most like to see. She was my favorite. I wish I had told her that. We read Richard Brautigan's poetry together and spent hours at the used bookstore down the street from Kent State University before heading to a coffee shop where we scrawled lines from our favorite poems on the walls of the bathroom.

She and I were seventeen together, and now her seventeen-year-old boy is dead.

His death weighs on me in a way that I did not anticipate.

Whether it is because he used a gun, or just because I can't reconcile the idea of a woman with whom I was a girl grieving the death of her boy, I don't know.

I start texting her a picture every day. Usually they're pictures from Africa—the roadside sign demarcating the Tropic of Capricorn, a seal snoozing in a giant tire in Cape Town's harbor, a weaver bird nest in Namibia. I hope that they are a tiny distraction. She tells me they are.

I don't even know my friend's child, but I'm so angry at him. How dare he end his life like this, leaving his mother in such a cataclysm of grief and guilt? Leaving his brother to become a man without him? What could possibly have been so awful that seventeen years on earth was enough? *Holocaust survivors have lived through more, you little shit*, I want to yell at him, stunned by my own presumption and superiority, that I am entitled to tell this child I don't even know, that life is worth living. Who am I to make that argument? Haven't I been there too, understanding perhaps just a shadow of what he must have felt? What transformation did he seek that could only be found in death? What was he running toward, instead of away from?

David Lester reflects that we must understand an individual's choices around death as an extension of his choices around life. He writes, "It is useful to remember that suicide can be a search for meaning, a search for rebirth, a search for God, and a search for spirituality. To simply dismiss it as a sin and an addiction to death misses the deep soul-searching that sometimes precedes such a destructive act."

"Transformation begins at this point for which there is no hope," writes James Hillman. "Despair produces the cry for salvation, for which hope would be too optimistic, too confident. . . . Despair ushers in the death experience and is at the same time the requirement for resurrection."

By the grace of years, I can see now that what I really wanted on that October day in the doctor's office, and on that January night in my old house, was not to die but to halt the agony of my marriage ending, the drawn-out death-by-a-million-paper-cuts torture that was the result of my own inability to imagine the future. It was just that at those moments, the two seemed indissoluble. And if I had known how to use the gun in Tom's desk drawer? I try to imagine positioning the cold muzzle beneath my chin, fumbling with the chamber and killing or maiming myself out of ignorance as much as despair. I am sick to think that I might have pulled the trigger. I was ready to die, I thought, for a transformation, a crossing from a humiliated, thwarted, bitter woman to an indomitable, radiant soul.

In all of us, always, maybe: there is the tug-of-war between rushing toward existence and rushing toward its end. It's much more comforting to believe in solid edges, a definite boundary between ourselves and others. *I am not like that. My son would never do that.* But what is more human than the yearning for transformation? It starts so young: playing dress-up, a costume on Halloween, trying on one persona at school and another at church, a tattoo. The "not-me" has to die in order that the "me" may fledge.

We are all so close to the edge, so perilously alike. We aren't safe in our own imaginations, let alone in the world. It might be our child who picks up the gun and aims it at his classmates, or himself.

It might be us.

Men Appear to Me as Monsters

ON OCTOBER 28, 2022, James and Jennifer Crumbley, the parents of a fifteen-year-old school shooter, were formally charged in Michigan for involuntary manslaughter. They had bought their son a Sig Sauer 9mm semiautomatic pistol the previous November, as an early Christmas present. He used it to murder four classmates (*Hana, Madisyn, Tate, Justin*). Their son pled guilty to multiple charges of first-degree murder, assault with intent to murder, and terrorism.

The Crumbleys' mug shots are often placed side by side, a triptych of mussed, sullen resentment.

A family.

I WAS NINETEEN the first time I went to a funeral for a friend. The summer after my first year of college, my high school class president, a boy named Scott—gregarious, athletic, bright, friendly—died of natural causes while on a summer internship in Colorado. It's a cliché to say that he was the popular guy who everyone liked, but he was the popular guy who everyone liked. Scott was an only child. I came home from my summer job one night and my parents told me the news. I ran, weeping, to a friend's house. A few days later, we attended the funeral together. It was the first time someone our age had died.

More than twenty years later, I still remember Scott's mother walking down the aisle of Holy Family Church, supported by her husband on one side and Scott's father on the other. I remember the rictus of grief on her face, paralyzed by the shock of attending her own child's funeral. After the service, I shook hands with Scott's father and stepfather, and hugged his mother, telling her, "I'm so proud to be able to say I knew him." I remember how thin she felt, not like an adult at all. Her body trembled as she hugged me back. I could not recall an adult ever holding on to me that way, as though I, a teenager, was the one giving comfort. I had a strange, inchoate awareness that I was seeing an adult who had become completely unmoored by, as Jon Krakauer writes, "a sense of loss so huge and irreparable that the mind balks at taking its measure."

DURING MY SABBATICAL at the University of the Free State, a South African colleague asked what was known about the parents of school shooters. I didn't have an answer. One might think that given the frequency of school shootings in the U.S., there would be reams of articles about parents, but there aren't. It is easy to pretend that school shooters emerge into the world as howling, murderous homunculi; however, their ordinariness gives the lie to our stereotypes. As Lucinda Roy, who tutored the Virginia Tech shooter, writes ruefully, "'we' are always 'they' in the end."

But.

When the Crumbleys heard that there had been a shooting at their son's school (where they had been summoned, just that day, because their son was drawing pictures of a gun and writing "Blood everywhere Help me" on his homework), "they fled their home on East Street—now a crime scene—for a hotel. Upon learning that they were also to be charged, they holed up in an artist's studio in a Detroit warehouse belonging to one of Jennifer's acquaintances and stopped responding to phone calls. Prosecutors say they had four burner phones (one they'd tried to destroy), four gift cards, ten credit cards, and $6,600 in cash. They had cleaned out [their son's] bank account."

I OFTEN TEACH *Frankenstein* in my college composition classes. So many students come into *Frankenstein* with preconceptions of the story—not the least of which is that Frankenstein is the Creature, not the scientist—but they are surprised by how it can be read as a parable about parents, children, and families. I tell them about Mary Shelley's shocking number of miscarriages and child deaths, how Percy Shelley once brought her a block of ice to sit on, to staunch the bleeding.

Victor Frankenstein is devastated by his mother's early death. He rails against the injustice of mortality: "I need not describe the feelings of those whose dearest ties are rent by that most irreparable evil," he thinks. Death is not the inevitable, unifying end to all life, but *evil*. Thus his fatal trajectory is set; he will reanimate life and become a god on his own terms: "A new species would bless me as its creator and source; many happy and excellent natures would owe their being to me. No father could claim the gratitude of his child so completely as I should deserve theirs."

After countless hours scouring charnel houses and cemeteries for body parts, his Creature is complete. But when light
enlivens the Creature's eyes, and his hand stretches out in affection to take Victor's, Frankenstein literally runs out of the
room in horror, repulsed by the Creature's appearance. My
students are bewildered by this. "If he wanted a pretty monster, he should have used prettier parts," they've said, or more
bluntly, "That's messed up." Frankenstein's rejection, and
countless subsequent rejections, ignite the Creature's indignant rage. "Beware; for I am fearless, and therefore powerful," the Creature warns. "I will watch with the wiliness of a
snake, that I may sting with its venom. Man, you shall repent
of the injuries you inflict."

It's not until Frankenstein himself has suffered the losses
of his brother, servant, confidant, and wife that he's able to
articulate the hubris that led him. There are so many lessons
to take from the story, but for me the critical one is that we
are responsible for what we bring into the world: inventions,
art, children. We don't get to run away when our creations
don't turn out the way we imagined.

But.

"According to a prosecutor's motion, Jennifer told a friend
that 'her son's destiny is done and she has to take care of herself.'"

IN FEBRUARY 2016, Sue Klebold, mother of one of the Columbine murderers, spoke with Diane Sawyer on *20/20*. A
few years ago, she and her husband were profiled in a chapter
of Andrew Solomon's book *Far from the Tree: Parents, Children,
and the Search for Identity.* Solomon also interviewed Peter

Lanza, the Sandy Hook murderer's father, in the *New Yorker*, and explored these parents' labyrinthine journey through guilt, bafflement, and grief. I downloaded Klebold's new memoir a few days after it was released, and read it in three nights. I finished it in the morning, over a third cup of tea, and my last thought was that I had never read such a brutal, unflinching confession of unconditional love.

"Perhaps the immutable error of parenthood is that we give our children what we wanted, whether they want it or not," writes Solomon in *Far from the Tree*. "We heal our wounds with the love we wish we'd received, but are often blind to the wounds we inflict."

I watch Sue Klebold's interview with Sawyer. Before it begins, Klebold paces around the room amid the camera equipment and microphones. She has luminous white hair and a thin face with expressive dark eyes. I imagine what might be going through Klebold's mind, and what she may be feeling. She is caught in a futile web, it seems; regardless of what she says, there will always be people who condemn her for her very existence. Every word she utters might be construed as an excuse, a demand for unearned sympathy. No matter how humble she makes herself, she cannot escape that she is alive, and someone else's child is not.

I was a young graduate teaching assistant at Colorado State University in April 1999, when the calamity at Columbine unfolded an hour or so south of us. I remember coming home on the bus that day knowing only scraps of the story, watching the news, the teenagers streaming out of the building with their hands on their heads. Only a year removed from my own freshmen students.

I think of the language that some people use to describe mass shooters: *monster*, *it*, the same words that Frankenstein uses to describe his creation. "Monster" comes from a Latin root, *monere*, to warn. There's a naïve bravado in that definition, implying that in every peril, there is an unambiguous CAUTION sign telling us to slow down and pay attention. In her book, Klebold writes, "Like all mythologies, this belief that Dylan was a monster served a deeper purpose: people needed to believe they would recognize evil in their midst. Monsters are unmistakable; you would know one if you saw one, wouldn't you?"

Instead, Klebold turns the tables on everyone who read about Columbine and thought *What kind of mother are you*, or *I would know if my kid were that fucked up*. Consider the opprobrium to which Klebold opens herself. She recounts all the missed opportunities to ask the right questions, all the warning lights that flickered in the dark. She forces readers to acknowledge that shooters also have families; they are someone's children, and their births were welcomed with the same joy and hope of any innocent victim. She admits to loving a mass murderer. In a sentence from Solomon's book that cracks my heart open, Klebold reflects, "It would have been better for the world if Dylan had never been born, but I believe it would not have been better for me."

After the wrongful execution of their servant, Justine Moritz, Victor Frankenstein's fiancée Elizabeth laments, "Before, I looked upon the accounts of vice and injustice that I read in books or heard from others as tales of ancient days or imaginary evils; at least they were remote and more familiar to reason than to the imagination; but now misery has come home, and men appear to me as monsters thirsting for each other's blood."

What hubris it is to believe that we can all see the monster coming, and get out of its way in time.

TWO MONTHS after my shooting, I went to the county courthouse for the shooter's pre-trial hearing. After passing through the metal detector, I found my way upstairs to the hearing chamber. Both wounded victims were there, as were other members of the campus community and media. Once inside, the shooter waived his right to the hearing, so it ended as quickly as it began. This meant that a grand jury would convene later in the fall. The judge left the room, the shooter exited, and those of us from the college entered a smaller antechamber where a court-appointed advocate explained how the next phases would proceed.

As I was walking back toward the elevator, I saw a small cluster of people coming out of the courtroom. A colleague nudged me. "Those are his parents," she whispered. They clutched each other's arms and trudged toward the elevator. I will never forget how ordinary they looked, his mother tired and blond, his father too small for his sport coat. There was nothing about their appearance that would reveal their son was capable of committing a school shooting. They looked haggard, drawn, hopeless.

During the initial phase of the shooter's case, it emerged that he had struggled with mental illness for years and had been, until shortly before the shooting, under the care of a psychiatrist. He had attempted suicide. His parents knew he was disturbed and had gotten him help. They just never dreamed he would hurt others; they thought he was only a danger to himself. Like Klebold, they are burdened with the whole knowledge of their failure.

"ALAS!" says Victor Frankenstein, "I had turned loose into the world a depraved wretch, whose delight was in carnage and misery."

WHEN WE LABEL someone a monster, our label filters back generations; it doesn't stick merely to the target of our condemnation. The rescindment of humanity becomes retroactive. Only monsters can create other monsters. By indicting shooters as subhuman, or inhuman, we are also indicting their families for creating them out of the same innocence and hope that every victim and perpetrator is created, denying them the grief that we can scarcely imagine.

In her book, Klebold recounts the tiny funeral they held for her son, and reflects that it was the last moment they would all be together as a family. Other shooters' families have secret ceremonies; in the *New Yorker* interview, Andrew Solomon asks Peter Lanza about what was done regarding his son's funeral, and Lanza replies, "No one knows that. And no one ever will." The other Columbine killer's gravesite is unknown, as is the Virginia Tech shooter's. It makes sense for their graves or interment sites to be concealed, to prevent them from becoming sites of perverted pilgrimage. But the phrase "secret funeral" sticks with me. What is a funeral, really, but proof that someone's life was more than the sum of all their days? I think back to my friend Scott's funeral, which demonstrated to his family that he was dearly loved. It assured them that they had been good parents; the turnout of mourners was proof that they had raised a solid kid. They had a final public affirmation that his life, though dreadfully short, had pulsed with meaning and connection.

The parents of killers bear grief that's amplified by the knowledge that their child will forever be known by only one act. As Peter Lanza says, "there could be no remembering who he was outside of who he became." They are denied the lines of friends who tell funny stories of their children, the teachers who remember them with fondness or exasperation. My high school English teacher read a poem at Scott's funeral: *"I'll lend you for a time a little child of mine, He said / For you to love the while he lives and mourn for when he's dead."* There are no poems to comfort the parents of a murderer. I know there are some who think that's how it should be, that shooters forfeited any right to be remembered with affection. But watching Sue Klebold wrestle with the truth of who her son was—and the endless suffering that I sense my shooter's parents also carry—prevents me from expelling them all from the greater human family.

I want to extend my hand to these forgotten parents. I give them permission, if I can, to remember their sons as the babies they once were, and to assure them that they have the right to mourn.

But.

"It was on a dreary night of November, that I beheld the accomplishment of my toils." And Frankenstein fled from the room when his Creation awoke.

It was on a dreary night of November, when a fifteen-year-old boy murdered four classmates. And his parents, too, fled, hiding in a studio loft with money and gift cards.

If *Frankenstein* is a horror story, as some argue, the horror comes from realizing that intent can be so violently disconnected from outcome, that your dream can change to nightmare in a second. The crucible into which we pour all our hopes and aspirations can very easily spill over with woe.

Sue Klebold has found a way to live with the agony, shame, and alienation of that otherness, and still retain the full measure of her son. She will not reject him, and though she writes that her love for Dylan did not save him, I suspect that it might have saved her.

Victor Frankenstein succeeded in defeating death. He created a new human being, as though he were God. He could not, though, love his Creation.

The three members of the Crumbley family have not seen one another since the shooting.

Postscript:

In December 2023, Ethan Crumbley was sentenced to life in prison without parole. In February 2024, his mother Jennifer Crumbley was convicted of four counts of involuntary manslaughter; in March 2024, his father James Crumbley was also convicted of four counts of involuntary manslaughter. They have each been sentenced to 10-15 years in prison.

Security Theater

"It is fear that rules this land."
—Alan Paton

ON THE DAY OF MY SHOOTING, my father is driving down from Ohio to visit me, stopping in Blacksburg overnight on his way to the Outer Banks. My sisters and mother try to get through to him on the way so that he knows what he's going to find, but of course, dads: he doesn't answer his cell phone. After driving me back to work that evening to see if I can get my school bag, purse, and laptop, we find the building wrapped in yellow crime scene tape. We go out for Mexican food.

I'm shoveling chips and salsa into my mouth, and I order a beer.

"May I see some ID?" asks the waitress.

"No," I tell her. "There was a shooting at my workplace today and my ID is locked in the building. Please, I would really like a beer."

She shakes her head regretfully, and I repeat my plea, in Spanish, and she is sorry, but they cannot serve me without identification. She summons a manager, who is also sorry that they cannot serve me without identification. My dad tells them how old I am, citing the circumstances of my birth: late March 1975, Ohio snowstorm! He shows them *his* driver's license, claiming that his age makes it impossible for me to be younger than twenty-one. But they don't budge. He lets me have a swig of his Pacifico when it arrives.

I am thirty-eight years old sitting in a Mexican restaurant with my seventy-three-year-old father and I can't have a beer because I can't prove I am over twenty-one because my driver's license is locked in the building where I survived a shooting four hours ago.

NINETEEN CHILDREN AND TWO TEACHERS were murdered in an elementary school in Uvalde, Texas, in May 2022. There was, as I expected, an initial flurry of details, with praise heaped on the Border Patrol officers who shot the perpetrator (is it worth saying, again, that he was a young alienated man with a history of sexual harassment who broadcast his plans on social media and bought his weapons legally? if only there were a pattern), but within days it emerged that the police waited more than an hour to "engage" the murderer.

"The officers waited, the report found, even as at least one high-ranking official—the acting chief of the Uvalde Police Department—learned that a teacher was wounded but still alive and that a child had been calling 911 for help from inside the classrooms. The committee found that none of the officers who learned of the calls advocated for 'shifting to an active shooter-style response or otherwise acting more urgently to breach the classrooms.'"

I knew that the sounds I heard on April 12, 2013, were gunshots. I knew, and I got my students out.

If I knew, they must have known.

How did I know, and act, and they did not?

"The [Uvalde] district said it was fortifying campuses with new eight-foot fences, security cameras, replacement door locks and additional police officers. Gov. Greg Abbott said he had assigned more than 30 state troopers to provide extra security."

THE FIRST TIME I went to South Africa in 2007, I was perplexed by the security apparatus in homes, hotels, and guest houses alike. I didn't know anyone in the U.S. who had an alarm system, nor did I know anyone whose house had been burgled. I had friends in Vermont who didn't even know where their house keys were; they regularly left their homes unlocked even while they were away on vacation. I had never seen anything like the sliding steel gates at the top of South African driveways, crowned with menacing sharp points to discourage climbers. I had never seen electric fencing atop ten-foot brick walls encircling a house. There were signs everywhere for private security companies and "armed response" teams. This was commonplace, in wealthy neighborhoods and middle-class ones alike. Even in the more impoverished townships, schools were guarded like fortresses and modest homes protected behind smaller, lower walls. I remember commenting on this to some of the local Fulbright staff, who were incredulous to hear that no neighborhood where I had lived in the U.S. had similar security. "So someone could just walk right up to your front door?" they asked. *Yes*, I replied. They clutched each other's arms and collapsed in laughter.

I knew, intellectually, the statistics about crime there. Rape in South Africa is horrifically frequent. There are intersections all over the country, in suburban, rural, and urban areas alike where it's acceptable not to come to a full stop after dark; such corners are often marked with a sign reading "Hi-Jacking Hotspot." Even Johan, early in our relationship, was robbed at gunpoint, forced onto his kitchen floor with a pistol in his mouth while a group of thieves ransacked his house for computers, firearms, and other valuables. I knew, as much as I could possibly understand from my vantage point, how deeply the fear of interpersonal and property crime penetrates all aspects of daily life.

And yet. In order to legally purchase a firearm there, you have to first complete a training course, certified by the government, and demonstrate proficiency with the weapon. You must undergo a psychological evaluation and submit character references. You must install a specific kind of gun safe, approved by South African Police Services, and your home will be inspected to ensure that the safe is up to standards. Then there is all the usual paperwork: background check, proof of residence and citizenship, fees. And then, finally, you can start the process of actually buying a gun.

Not once have any of my South African friends or family members said, "I wish our gun laws were more like yours."

The measures common in South Africa are all defensive, it seems to me: the locks, the gates, the alarms. The country has not responded to commonplace violent crime with sweeping statutes to arm the citizenry. It has not made murder in self-defense a legitimate, state-sanctioned response to fear.

WE ARE GOING TO HAVE more emergency drills this year. Whether they'll be active shooter, or general disaster drills, I don't know. I had never had a drill before my shooting. If I did the "right thing," it was by chance and instinct alone.

I can't sit through videos of active shooter events. Seven years ago, I was at a faculty leadership development seminar in Richmond, and during a segment about active shooters, the presenter's PowerPoint flashed a photo of me—of *me*—from the day of the shooting, standing outside my school, back to the camera, khaki jacket, hair falling out of a claw clip. I was a slide in someone's PowerPoint. The presenter didn't know that I was in the audience; they'd just pulled the image from the Internet. But to sit there, and see myself used as a visual aid in a presentation about active shooter events—

All of this is more than I can carry.

BECAUSE I AM AN ENGLISH PROFESSOR, I am always taking words apart, as though dismantling them will reveal something at the core. I want to believe that if I look hard enough I'll find a pure, sparkling truth. *Security* comes from Latin, *securus*; its meaning in the fifteenth century was "without care or fear, dreading no evil." Also "freedom from care or anxiety."

The motto of Montgomery County, Virginia, where I live, is "Freedom Increases Responsibility." In 2019 the Virginia General Assembly passed a slew of firearm regulations, and many counties responded by declaring themselves "Second Amendment sanctuaries," where none of the restrictions would be followed. The designation has no real power, but emotion does.

SANCTUARY: "consecrated place; place of refuge or protection"; from Latin *sanctus*, holy.

I spoke at another Board of Supervisors meeting: *My classroom should have been a sanctuary.*

AFTER THE MASSACRE in Uvalde, Texas, other school districts in Texas will be requiring kids to use only clear plastic backpacks. "The bags must be completely clear and not have a colored tint to them," NPR reported. "Middle schoolers' bags must not exceed 12 inches wide by 16.5 inches tall and 5 inches deep, while high schoolers' bags must not exceed 13 inches wide by 17.5 inches tall and 6.5 inches deep."

I would like to ask a child what she thinks of this solution.

That what she carries in her 12 x 16.5 x 5 clear plastic backpack (candy-scented hand sanitizer? earbuds? eraser? phone which she may have to use to call 911?) must be surveilled because adults cannot be asked to lock up their guns at home. That she must be literally transparent, her possessions scrutinized down to the tiniest dimension in the name of safety, which adults fail to provide. That her life must shrink, because adults cannot make decisions based on actual evidence. That adults have only rights, not responsibilities.

THE DEPARTMENT OF HOMELAND SECURITY allocated nearly two million dollars in 2018 for high schools to train students to treat gunshot injury. "To deliver free to the public, lifesaving trauma training to high school students for mass casualty events," reads the grant description. A good idea, perhaps, because in 2021, at Oxford High School in Michigan, during a mass casualty event, a security officer thought that she was witnessing an active shooter drill and that one of the children who had been shot was simply wearing good makeup. She walked past him. He died.

I want to believe that underneath the casual violence of these policies, the resignation cloaked in words of power and care and control, is a terror so deep that the people cannot even look at it. The fear of the fear of their child's murder is titanic—it cannot be held in the mind's space. It can't be real, so no one can be made to act as though it is real.

The children are braver than the adults. This should break us all.

AS I NAVIGATE my dozen open research tabs, an ad pops up for a bullet-proof backpack manufacturer. "Our panels," the website claims, "are constructed using multiple layers of ballistic PE material that is a strong, synthetic PE fiber similar to Kevlar®. It is used in the global production of body armor, helmets, and ballistic vests, just to name a few. You can confidently depend on our panels for protection against all kinds of handgun bullets and fragments, as well as against stabbing with sharp and pointed objects."

I WAS OUT on the local walking trail with my dog last week when a college-age woman ran past us, fleet as a springbok, with a palomino-blonde ponytail flying behind her. I idly remembered an urban legend/admonition from college, that a long loose ponytail made it more possible for a rapist to grab you, so you should tie up your hair when you're running or walking alone. So many things for women to remember. Hold your keys with the points facing outward. Check under your car in a parking garage because there might be someone under there waiting to slice your Achilles tendons. Don't wear headphones because you won't be able to hear someone behind you. Don't run alone. Don't be afraid.

On July 31, 2022, the *New York Times* published a long article about new regulations in Ohio that allow teachers to carry guns after twenty-four hours of training. The location is noted as Rittman, Ohio, a town not far from where I grew up and went to college. The central figure in the story is Mandi, a kindergarten teacher training to carry a concealed gun in her classroom.

"Studies on school employees carrying guns have been limited," the article reads, "and research so far has found little evidence that it is effective. There is also little evidence that school resource officers are broadly effective at preventing school shootings, which are statistically rare. Yet arming school employees is finding appeal—slight majorities among parents and adults in recent polls."

Research has found little evidence that it is effective.

Could there be a more fitting sentiment for virtually everything related to American gun culture?

A way to reframe this is to say that Ohio has now empowered teachers to legally kill children, because most school shooters are students.

To do the jobs of law enforcement because law enforcement cannot be trusted to serve and protect. To do the jobs of school security officers who can't tell the difference between good makeup and blood. To do the jobs of so-called responsible gun owners, because most school shooters get their guns from home and adults did not secure them.

I think of the interviews I've had for teaching jobs in colleges and high school. I imagine being asked, *Are you willing to carry a gun? Would you be willing to shoot a student?*

Teachers are leaving the profession in droves, the national newspapers proclaim.

The children must wear clear backpacks, bulletproof backpacks, and learn to apply tourniquets. The teachers must carry guns. We must shift blame onto the innocent because the guilty refuse to bear anything. I imagine denial as a force so bright, so radiant with certainty that it incinerates everything in its path.

FEAR IS THE CURRENCY MOST SPENT IN AMERICA. This is something Johan has said over and over, an unwelcome realization from his first few years in the United States. I cannot wrap my head around American willingness to do literally anything other than address the actual problems: that there are more firearms than people in this country; that they are virtually unregulated; that the firearm industry is shielded from liability; that there is no culture of responsibility which would ensure that adults lock guns away from children. It would be farcical if it weren't life or death.

Sometimes I wonder if my rage is so constant that I don't even notice it anymore. I have stopped paying attention to the cost of saturating myself in this world of data about gun violence, knowing what every think tank and researcher finds, what so many citizens and politicians ignore.

I don't know how much longer I can write this book. It was not that hard to do the research; it has taken up much of my time and mental and emotional stamina, yes, but it is not impossible. The studies are out there. The data exists. I cannot understand why the people with power to do something simply will not do it. I don't understand how they can live. It's becoming almost impossible for me to persist in this intellectual and emotional space, where I know about what's true and what's not, what's supported by evidence and what's not, and yet the public conversations are dominated by the most outrageous, frenzied paranoia imaginable. I will never be done, I can never catch up, I cannot write fast enough to account for all the death. (As though I can stop people from dying by writing. Who do I think I am?)

I'M STILL GETTING CARDED regularly (most recently while purchasing nonalcoholic beer, of all things). I'm forty-nine. People tell me I should be flattered, it's a compliment that I look so young! It isn't. It is security theater. It's a waste of time, a stupid waste of time, and it's a symptom of a culture that invests a lot in the appearance of doing something about a problem, but behind closed doors has given up.

TODAY IS MARCH 19, 2024, and the Gun Violence Archive reports 6,031 firearm deaths and injuries so far this year. It will be more by the time this book goes to print. The number will lose all meaning if we do not turn on the spotlight and draw back the curtains.

I think it has already lost all meaning.

To the Third and Fourth Generations

Akron, Ohio: St Nicholas Orthodox Cemetery
In a shadow-dappled corner of this quiet cemetery, my paternal ancestors rest. Some of my grandfather's siblings and my father's godmother are buried there, as well as my great-grandparents Sophia and Adam, and my great-great-grandparents, Vasily and Mary. They came from a tiny village called Łosie, near the Poland-Ukraine border. How many weeks did the passage take, I wonder; how many ports did the ship call at before facing the cold Atlantic, before there was no turning back?

Many headstones in the Russian cemetery are inscribed with the broken Orthodox cross. Some have long epitaphs in elaborate Cyrillic. It is foreign, ornate, calligraphic: it activates some atavistic memory in me that aligns baroque chants, incense and icons, and esoteric rituals with holiness. I studied Russian for a year or so under the tutelage of a native speaker, and even now I love the cadence of it, overlapping sibilants and gentle, sighing diminutives. When they came to America, Vasily didn't let Mary learn English; she gave birth to their first child in this country alone, at home, because she could not go to anyone to ask for help.

I never knew the people buried in that corner, without whom I would not exist. I hope, though, that if they can see me, that they are proud. That Mary, my twice-great-grand-mother, might thrill to hear my voice in the language she could not learn, might love to hear me stumbling through the language of her birth.

As I WRITE this chapter, the sound of a gunshot ejects me from my chair. My heart stops; my dog Amber springs from her bed and cowers under my desk. My husband has just come home, and I stare out the window at his car, terrified, for a second, that he has shot himself. There is no reason for me to fear this: he does not have a gun, has shown no sign that he wants to kill himself, but it is the first thing I think of.

The neighborhood is quiet and torpid in July heat. The front door squeaks. I rush to the kitchen to make sure he is alive, and I hear him crooning to greet Amber. I try to hide my face. I'm embarrassed for him to see my fear. He heard the sound too. *No*, he says of the sound, *that was too blunt. A firecracker, not a firearm.*

Are you sure? *Yes.*

I will never be sure again.

WINTER IN NAZI-OCCUPIED HOLLAND. People were starving. They ate sugar beets, beechnuts, and tulip bulbs to survive. The Amsterdam I gleefully traipsed with my girlfriends in 2015 was a vivid garden full of green-sap life and clear water running in the streams of the Vondelpark. Amsterdam in 1944 was a wasteland of frozen canals and skeletal trees. By the time of liberation in May 1945, more than twenty thousand Dutch citizens had died of starvation. There were pregnant women that year, as there were all over the world. The Dutch women's babies, though, bore imprints of their mothers' hunger. They were born more prone to obesity and metabolic dysfunction.

Historical trauma broadly refers to mass traumatic suffering passed down through generations as a collective psychic response to the "soul wound" of colonization, assimilation, and extermination. It is the "incomplete mourning and resulting depression absorbed by children from birth onward." If "the body keeps the score," as Bessel van der Kolk writes, the bodies of the pregnant women and their babies are palimpsests of emptiness and bounty, each calorie and vitamin scrupulously accounted for. "The intergenerational transmission of trauma reveals the degree to which persons can bear each other's experiences and bear them not cognitively, but somatically."

TEN YEARS AGO, if I thought of gun violence at all, it was as of a bullet: small, smooth-edged, self-contained. It had a traceable path with delineated edges. It could be identified and collected as a discrete piece of evidence. I did not comprehend the literal and metaphorical power contained in that tiny shell. Now I see the aftermath: the fragments and shards that splinter off and embed in every muscle and memory.

I have emigrated to this foreign country, which I can't even name: Survivorland? Schoolshootingland? I know nothing of the ships, the timetables, the ports that brought my ancestors to the United States but I can tell you the date, the time, the distance that I traveled (two o'clock in the afternoon on Friday, April 12, 2013; twelve steps to cross from the instructor console to the door once we heard the first shot, pause, two more, then my students and I took flight). I have lived here now for ten years. It is not the country I think my ancestors anticipated.

MY FRIEND M. witnessed the 2007 massacre at Virginia Tech from her office in an adjacent building. Like me, she is still haunted by anxiety, nightmares, panic attacks—the sticky residue of that day cannot be rinsed off. She is interviewed for a feature in the *New York Times* about parenting. She tells of calling her own father from lockdown, as she listened to the barrage of gunfire in the building next door. *There's no way it could be only one shooter*, she thought, no way that one person and one weapon could unleash such violence. She tells of watching bodies of the injured assisted out of the building. The bodies of the dead would remain there for another twenty-four hours. A chilling detail learned later, from first responders, was the building's ghastly silence except for the sounds of dozens of cell phones, cell phones of the dead and injured, ringing, ringing, ringing.

Years later M.'s son, upon learning of the Parkland massacre, asks in astonishment, "That couldn't happen here, could it, Mom?" and that is how she must tell him the story of what happened in his own town, to his own mother. Although symbols of the massacre exist in slogans on T-shirts, like WE WILL PREVAIL and WE ARE VIRGINIA TECH, the massacre itself is rarely spoken of. The scar is praised; the wound is hidden.

M.'s boy sees people carrying guns in the supermarket

(legal in Virginia) and he panics, telling her that they have to leave NOW. She wonders if she passed something on to him, whether her own memories and anguish have shaped this boy, her oldest. "What do you say when the boogeyman is real?" she asks.

The fathers ate sour grapes and their children's teeth were set on edge (Ezekiel 18:2).

The mothers watch a massacre, and their children tremble.

I'M WAITING at the self-checkout kiosk at the library in Blacksburg, Virginia. If you draw a line between Norris Hall on the Virginia Tech campus, where the worst of the rampage took place, and my campus, five miles away, where our rampage took place six years later, the library lies in between. A teenage boy in another queue has downcast eyes, his hands kneading deep in his hoodie pockets. Pockets deep enough to conceal a gun. Every ligament in my body alights as if a match has been struck and I'm ready to tackle him when he withdraws the gun that he'll use to kill us all.

It's only a black nylon wallet, after all. In this country, the one where I live now, a wallet might be a gun. A boy might open fire. This is not the country I think my ancestors anticipated.

THIS MAY SOUND like a time-travel paradox, but I am the third generation of childless eldest daughters, on my mother's side. My great-aunt Isabelle, whom I remember mostly as a somnolent, cantankerous figure, was the oldest of four girls. My mother's mother, Eva May, was the third of those four, and the only one who married and had children. Eva May's first daughter, Linda, my mother's older sister, had no children. She was an English teacher, too. And me—my mother's oldest, all of us educators, travelers, aunts only. Only.

I did not see myself in them when I was young. I didn't see what it might have cost my great-grandparents to educate four girls during the Depression or what my great-aunts might have felt deprived of as single women in the 1950s and '60s. In my memories of them, I summon pastel trousers and matching shirts; kaleidoscopic glass paperweights scattered across the tables of their houses; fancy hat boxes; fox and mink stoles with the heads and paws still on. And a display case of decorative spoons that they'd collected from across the world.

I am an aunt to four, godmother to one, and I'm very taken with the idea of being a "good ancestor," a phrase I first encountered from the anti-racist writer and activist Layla Saad on Instagram. Perhaps it's because of the time I have spent in southern Africa, or the preoccupation with the people who came before me in my own lineage (all those graves), the women who chose something other than motherhood. I have never yearned for kids the way that, evidently, so many people do. Now more than ever, I am grateful that I never even felt that longing. One of my own wise women told me once that if you don't have children in this life, it's because you had too many in a previous incarnation. This time, you get to rest. You get to do something else.

All I want now, all I have ever wanted since the day I wrote "post-shooting lesson plans," was to be the last professor to create such a lunatic, incomprehensible document. So, this is what I get to do, in this life: write and try to convince people that it is indeed as bad as they can imagine. You do not want this way of being. You don't want to immigrate here.

"In the 20 years since Columbine, some 223,000 American students have been exposed to gun violence at 229 schools across the country, according to a database of gun violence compiled by the *Washington Post*. In terms of absolutes, those numbers may appear small: 3.3 million students are expected to graduate from public high schools this year alone, according to the National Center for Education Statistics. But school shootings don't just kill and maim: They traumatize and terrorize, and the wounds they leave cast long scars across American civil society." This was published in the *Pacific Standard* in 2019. Those numbers are already irrelevant. (And notice the absence of educators in that statement, as though all those kids were in class alone. The elision of people like me is another constant, aching absence. We too have families and friends, we too deserve to be remembered.)

Even if a bullet is not designed to be hollow-pointed and explode on impact, it does. It doesn't destroy just a limb, organ, body. It steals wholeness, coherence, the ability to trust the banality of noise and, worst, the power of language. There are no neat beginning and ending lines here: memory, guilt, shame, grief, loss, terror, voicelessness bleed into the present, defying the solidity of brick or glass.

Natan P. F. Kellermann employs the phrase "catastrophic expectancy" as a cognitive characteristic of the children of Holocaust survivors: a conviction that recurrence is certain. In 2021, a man opened fire on a Boulder, Colorado, supermarket, killing ten people. One of the witnesses said, "It seemed like all of us had imagined we'd be in a situation like this at some point in our lives."

This is why I am certain that I will be shot and killed. The tightening circle of school shootings in my life can only end one way. Dunblane, Columbine, Virginia Tech, my school. It gets closer and closer. I get closer to the center. The bullet will find me eventually.

David Morris, in *The Evil Hours: A Biography of Post-Traumatic Stress Disorder*, writes "It is, perhaps, the fatal flaw of humankind, this failure to learn from conflict. . . . [I]f a 'cure' for post-traumatic stress disorder can be found, then society as a whole won't have to bother with trying to deal with the events that cause trauma, which have deep roots in social justice issues."

HAVE WE LEARNED NOTHING about the way trauma, violence, scarcity, dispossession, and peril infect each generation?

NOT FOR THE FIRST TIME am I grateful that I have no children. What I am now, what I have become, should not be anyone's inheritance.

Braddock, Pennsylvania: Monongahela Cemetery

These are my mother's people: my great-grandparents George (Juraj, *YOU-rye*) and Elizabeth (Alzbeta, *ALZ-beata*). This cemetery was once known for being the final resting place of many of Pittsburgh's Slovakian immigrants. My people's headstones are clouded with gray-green moss, wet and cold on this late March day.

I crouch in the rain before them.

My paperwork says they came from Kosice, Slovakia. When I look at pictures of the city, I see a fairy tale of sinuous cobbled streets, a castle, a singing fountain. I look at these pictures and wonder why they left to become miners and bricklayers and housekeepers in Pennsylvania. Did they dream of home? Were they glad to leave it behind? How long did it take them to start dreaming in English?

What did they imagine that I would inherit?

I speak English and I do so with joy, reveling in the words and poetry of what is now my own mother tongue. I have all the education they never had. I am a professor, a writer. I have seen so much of the world; I have one foot on another continent. I am what they hoped for.

And yet: in my own classroom in rural Virginia, my students and I ran from a man with a shotgun.

THIS ESSAY, this book: these are the only legacies I can leave.

Sweet, Quiet Boys;
or, Divinities Implacable

"We are gratified by the public comments made by other Santa Fe High School students that show [shooter] as we know him: a smart, quiet, sweet boy."

THIS WEEK it is a man in Uniontown, Ohio, near where I grew up. His wife's coworker called for a welfare check after she did not show up for work. Officers found the entire family—father, mother, three children: ages fifteen, twelve, and nine—shot to death. What I always think of, in these stories, is that the last thing the children saw in life was their father, shooting them.

I TAKE THE WORD APART like a surgeon:
    annihilate: "reduce to nothing." From Latin *ad*, to; and *nihil*, nothing.
A family annihilator, then, reduces his family to nothing.

FAMILY ANNIHILATIONS happen every five days.

NOVEMBER 2014/February 2018/May 2018/November 2021/May 2022

There is a shooting at _____school.

I instantly surmise three things:

one, that the shooter is male;
two, that the first victim is female;
and three, that the shooter has brought the gun from home.

I have been right on all three counts dozens of times since.

Usually, I love being the smartest girl in the room. Not anymore. Instead of pride and glee, knowledge ignites me with fury.

Gun violence is like the tower viewers at scenic overlooks. Insert a quarter and you can scan the whole horizon, things coming into vivid focus. Zero in on one shooting, and you will see a boy or a man at the center with a woman's body on the ground. Pull back, wider and wider, and you will see a crowd of men surrounded by graveyards of women.

South African writer and scholar Njabulo Ndebele, writing about the spectacular, reflects, "What is finally left and what is deeply etched in our minds is the spectacular contest between the powerless and the powerful."

Look at me.

I was having a bad week, my shooter told police, when they asked him why he opened fire at our school (male shooter, female victims).

WOMEN DO NOT COMMIT rampage shootings because we are angry at how our culture ignores, silences, and diminishes us, or because we have bad weeks.

It's curious, isn't it? Because don't we have reason to act out this way? Don't women have legitimate grievances that would, if not justify such violence, at least make it understandable? Has no one noticed that women and girls also play violent video games? And take psychiatric medications? And are romantically rejected? And have unfettered access to firearms? And grow up in homes without fathers? And get fired from their jobs? And have bad days and weeks and years?

IN JANUARY 2023, it was a man in Utah. He shot and killed his wife, his mother-in-law, his seventeen-year-old daughter, his thirteen-year-old daughter, his seven-year-old twins (boy and girl), and his four-year-old son. And then himself.

His wife had just filed for divorce.

The funeral home obituary for the murderer drew comments like these:

[Murderer's name] . . . was always kind and good to us and always was willing to lend a helping hand. We don't know the whys and how's but I do know it's not our right to judge. And the Lord loves [murderer] very much.

I'm grateful for his example of Christlike love and service.

THE FURIAE, OR ERINYES, are the Greek goddesses of vengeance. They are called the Night-Born Sisters. Snakes undulate in their hair. They guard the dungeons of the damned, but come forth to punish murderers. Allecto, unceasing.

Megaera, grudging. Tisiphone, avenging murder.

Their name is ancient, from *erinuô:* I am angry.

I relish the story that they grew from drops of the blood spattered when their father Uranus was castrated by his son, Kronos.

Once, I was afraid of my own fury. It swelled and pulsed through my veins and pounded in my brain and I used to run and run as far and fast as I could just to flatten it, to exhaust it, so that I would feel something, anything, else.

But now it is a friend, it is familiar, it is icy and righteous and I will no longer try to pray it away.

In *Metamorphoses*, Ovid writes: "Malign Tisiphone seized a torch steeped in blood, put on a robe all red with dripping gore and wound a snake about her waist."

Look at me.

The rage I feel at this country which never ever calls it out, refuses to name what is so glaring to me and to literally anyone who pays a scintilla of attention: that rage is exhausting.

The rage at the follow-up news story about the man in Utah: In 2020 he was investigated for domestic abuse, he choked their fourteen-year-old daughter, he took his wife's devices to spy on her messages. He took away all the family's guns, for himself. But, *his Christlike love and service.*

The annihilation is never the first sign that something was wrong. It's the last.

I shouldn't be surprised, I guess, that men so indignantly resist the very idea that firearm violence may have something to do with masculinity. Then they might have to ask whether the men they know have ever been abusive, or raped someone. Then they might have to ask if they, themselves, have ever been abusive, or raped someone. (Because every woman knows a woman who has been raped but no men know a rapist.)

Then they might have to act.

How much energy all the women I know have expended, trying to create bubbles of protection around our bodies: cultivating brisk strides, parking under lights, carrying pepper spray, always trying to stay one step ahead of the men who would harass and rape and kill us. What might we do if we could direct that energy elsewhere?

What would the United States look like if women killed every man who made them fear for their lives?

Is this why men kill us so frequently? Because they know what the streets would look like if we did it?

I wish I knew the invocation that would summon the Furies. *Erinuô.*

Especially Tisiphone. Retribution.

The man who murdered seven people in Isla Vista, California, in 2014 left behind a blood-freezing manifesto in which he chronicled every injustice done to him by the women in his life: his mother, his classmates, the nameless girls who strolled around town, heedless of his burning ~~desire~~ right to fuck them.

"I concluded that women are flawed," he wrote. "There is something mentally wrong with the way their brains are wired, as if they haven't evolved from animal-like thinking. Women are like a plague that must be quarantined. When I came to this brilliant, perfect revelation, I felt like everything was now clear to me, in a bitter, twisted way. I am one of the few people on this world who has the intelligence to see this. I am like a god, and my purpose is to exact ultimate Retribution on all of the impurities I see in the world."

Imagine how differently we would respond if his name had been Ellie, and her manifesto had said:

"I concluded that men are flawed. There is something mentally wrong with the way their brains are wired, as if they haven't evolved from animal-like thinking. Men are like a plague that must be quarantined. When I came to this brilliant, perfect revelation, I felt like everything was now clear to me, in a bitter, twisted way. I am one of the few people on this world who has the intelligence to see this. I am like a goddess, and my purpose is to exact ultimate Retribution on all of the impurities I see in the world."

"No prayer, no sacrifice, and no tears can move [the Furies], or protect the object of their persecution."

Make no mistake; if Ellie had left behind that manifesto, our national conversation about gun violence would relentlessly interrogate femininity, women's anger, and revenge.

In the *Metamorphoses*, Juno implores the Furies to punish a king and queen whose preening pride has insulted her. She journeys on a "downward path, gloomy with fatal yew trees: it leads through dumb silence to the infernal regions," where she summons the Furies from the depths of Hell and requests vengeance upon those who have wronged her. *Consider it done*, says Tisiphone. Brandishing a torch and wearing a viper around her waist, she goes forth with Grief, Panic, Terror, and Madness at her side. "Stretching out her arms, wreathed with knots of vipers, she flailed her hair, and the snakes hissed at her movements. Some coiled over her shoulders, some slid over her breast, giving out whistling noises, vomiting blood, and flickering their tongues."

Someday, Ellie will commit a mass shooting in a male-dominated venue: a gun show, a sporting event, Congress. How will we respond when she leaves behind YouTube videos and a manifesto detailing repeated assaults by a male relative, or rape at the hands of a "friend," or humiliating, victim-blaming skepticism from police? What if she recounts every single catcall, every uninvited grope, every obscene gesture, and every sexist comment she has ever received? What if she describes how an ex-partner posted intimate pictures of her on the Internet without her consent? What if she describes being stalked by an ex-partner and dismissed for being overly cautious? What if she details the times she was silenced in a meeting at work, chastised for being too emotional, asked if she was on the rag? What if she rails at society for claiming her body as public property? What if she decides that her only recourse, her only way to reclaim power, is to pick up a gun and enact revenge on all the men who used their social privilege and physical size to remind her that she was a woman, and therefore always less?

Tisiphone flings poisonous fluid at her victims, "those that cause vague delusions, dark oblivions of the mind, wickedness and weeping . . . [s]he had boiled them, mixed with fresh blood, in hollow bronze, stirred with a stalk of green hemlock." Then she sets them on fire.

A conflagration reeking of testosterone, blood, metal, and flesh, of entitlement and gleeful mockery: how lovely.

Reduced to nothing.

Just Another Week in 2022

May 15, 2022: South Africa

I have already reached for my phone when Johan shouts at me, *Don't read the news!* I have just seen Ibram Kendi's Instagram post, and though I don't know the story, I know the story. I go to the *New York Times* app. This time, ten people are dead and three injured at a Tops supermarket in Buffalo, New York. All of them were Black. The young white male shooter live-streamed the massacre. He left behind a white supremacist manifesto.

The dead victims' names are Aaron, Celestine, Roberta, Andre, Katherine, Margus, Heyward, Geraldine, Ruth, and Pearl.

YESTERDAY we drove back to our Airbnb in Pretoria from Pilanesberg National Park in the North West province. I gazed up at the craggy, red-rock aloe-speckled slopes of the Magaliesberg range, the blond savannas as the land flattened out, endless fields of sunflowers tilting their faces to the equally endless sky. We drove through a township with a strip mall of its own. A supermarket, sports betting parlor, barber. Kids gathered in the middle of the road holding up signs asking for donations to their football club, for uniforms, for cleats. As cars slowed to negotiate the potholes in the road, a group rushed each car, the children's beautiful guileless smiles aglow.

I thought of that supermarket, the parking lot crowded with cars, car guards in fluorescent vests strolling the rows, pocketing a few rand here and there as people pulled out, children literally standing in the middle of a four-lane highway. I thought that of all the things those people might have been worrying about that day, a furious young white man with an AR-15 was low on the list.

So many mass murders in the United States, with few exceptions, are sadly predictable. Was it ever a real doubt in anyone's mind that the shooter was male? That if he was white, he was arrested, not killed by police? That he acquired his guns legally? That he was "motivated" by a feverish belief in white replacement theory, "a conspiracy theory that states that nonwhite individuals are being brought into the United States and other Western countries to 'replace' white voters to achieve a political agenda. . . . White supremacists argue that the influx of immigrants, people of color more specifically, will lead to the extinction of the white race"?

American news outlets always fall all over themselves earnestly inquiring what the murderer's motive might be. I am so tired of this. I can't stand the breathless, baffled tone as though we have never seen anything like this before.

He wanted to, and he could. It's really not confusing.

WHEN I LIVED in Bloemfontein, I used to take the Intercape bus to Centurion, where Johan lived. The trip took about six hours. I was rarely the only white person on the bus, but white people were always in the minority. I loved the double-decker buses with televisions and seats that reclined. Intercape's website says, "It is our firm belief that God's purpose for our company is to be more than just a carrier of passengers. It is our joy and privilege to be a carrier of the good news that Jesus Christ saves, and to bring His hope to the nation and the continent," which explained why the movie *God Is Not Dead* was always playing on the TV. We always stopped at a rest area in a town called Kroonvaal, where we dutifully disembarked to use the toilet, buy bags of Simba chips and Zoofari animal crackers, a bottle of poison-green Sparletta crème soda. On one trip I made friends with Gerald, who had boarded the bus in Cape Town and was traveling home to Zimbabwe for a funeral. We shared an apple, and he asked me to text his wife that he arrived at Park Station in Joburg safely, where he'd change buses for the route north.

IN THE UNITED STATES, white people are 61 percent of the population.

I wish I could ask white replacement theory believers what, exactly, would be so terrible about finally being the racial minority. What, exactly, do they think will happen?

I wonder if they can articulate their fear and their shame.

WRITING for *Harper's* in 2019, James Pogue describes a conversation with Simon Roche, an Afrikaner white nationalist, whose talk of put-upon whites echoes that of so much rhetoric in the U.S. "It's this resentment that connects him to other aggrieved whites across the world," Pogue reflects, "and it was striking to hear his words and think how comfortably they'd fit in the mouths of conservative friends of mine in the United States, talking about immigrants or Black Lives Matter."

June 27, 2022

Today, police in Akron, Ohio, killed twenty-five-year-old Jayland Walker. The details are emerging, but these are facts: Walker is Black, and was initially the subject of a traffic stop. He was shot more than sixty times by police as he was running away from them. They fired ninety-four shots in 6.7 seconds. A gun was found in Walker's car. Permitless carry went into effect in Ohio on June 13. There's been a curfew in place for the last few days because of demonstrations.

I was born in Akron and was baptized, raised, and married for the first time in a United Methodist church there. My grandparents, great-grandparents, and extended family are buried in various cemeteries throughout the city. A trip through Akron is a trip through all the neighborhoods where my father grew up in the 1940s and '50s. I look at the news reports from the local paper on the protests, and position them on my fading map of memory: *in front of a bookstore in Highland Square, officers in riot gear on High Street.* Streets I know.

ARCHBISHOP TREVOR HUDDLESTON spent much of his career ministering in Sophiatown township, outside Johannesburg. In his memoir *Naught for Your Comfort*, he wrote, "It is not crime that matters. It is control."

July 4, 2022

Today a twenty-one-year-old white man murdered seven people at a parade in Highland Park, Illinois. The details are emerging, but these are facts: The murderer is white. He used an AR-15, which he bought legally, despite the fact that in 2019, police had confiscated all his knives after he threatened to kill family members. The killer was arrested, alive, and will face trial.

HUDDLESTON WRITES, "Surely if the incarnation means anything at all, it must mean the breaking down of barriers not by words but by deed, by act, by *identification*. To accept racial discrimination . . . is a blasphemy against the Holy Spirit of God Himself."

A FEW YEARS AGO, I brought one of my advanced writing classes together with two sociology classes to hear Reverend Osagyefo Sekou speak; Sekou works regularly with Black Lives Matter, though he's not an official representative of the organization. The sociology students had prepared a list of questions to ask; he was Skyping in from near St. Louis. One question that emerged early was, "What is the ultimate goal of Black Lives Matter?"

Reverend Sekou paused, leaned toward the screen, and spoke firmly, enunciating every word.

"Stop killing us," he said.

When we debriefed the session the following class period, overwhelmingly, my class said they had found Sekou offensive and inappropriate (he used profanity throughout his conversation with us, which clearly conflicted with their sense of how a preacher should behave). They were angry about the perceived implication that cops are corrupt. They mounted the usual objections about all lives mattering, #notallcops; they never owned slaves so why should they be held responsible for the ills facing Black people today? Most shockingly, for me, was a student's remark that "life was pretty bad in Africa anyway," meaning that American slavery actually did Black people a favor.

THERE ARE A LOT OF THINGS I could say here about white fragility, perceptions of individual versus systemic racism, unquestioning righteousness of law enforcement, gross misunderstandings of history. In their childlike rejection of any implicit accountability, they forgot Rekia Boyd, Michael Brown, Philando Castile, Terence Crutcher, Jordan Edwards, John Crawford, Anthony Gray, Charleena Lyles, Tamir Rice, Walter Scott, Alton Sterling, Marcus-David Peters, Breonna Taylor, Stephon Clark, Patrick Lyoya, and Jayland Walker.

All of them Black. None of them injured another person. All were shot and killed by police.

MY STUDENTS also forgot:

R. D., white, killed three, including a police officer. Arrested and stood trial.

J. H., white, killed twelve. Arrested and stood trial.

J. L. L., white, killed six people and severely wounded Congresswoman Gabrielle Giffords. Arrested and stood trial.

D. R., white, killed nine. Arrested and stood trial.

N. C., white, killed seventeen. Arrested and stood trial.

D. P., white, killed ten. Arrested and stood trial.

P. C., white, killed twenty-three. Arrested and stood trial.

And my shooter. White. Shot two people. Arrested and stood trial.

My students weren't wrong to point out that police risk their lives every day. But they forgot this: *mortal risk is part of that job.* You know that when you become a police officer. And I emphasize the word "become": it is a choice to become a police officer, hence the falseness of "Blue Lives Matter."

There are no blue lives because there are no blue people.

IN *THE SECOND: RACE AND GUNS IN A FATALLY UNEQUAL AMERICA*, Carol Anderson writes, "The key variable in the way that the Second Amendment operates is not guns but anti-Blackness."

I RETURN OVER AND OVER to the cost of firearm violence, paid in fear and early warning systems and destruction of trust in one another. I can focus with microscopic precision on the singularity of my own experience, the particular memories and burdens that I must carry. *Was April 12 the cost of teaching in the twenty-first century?* Pulling back, broadening the scope and looking at the entire American panorama of gun violence, particularly the use of deadly force against Black civilians, I ask other questions: *What is the cost to the countless other families of Black people killed by police who also saw the killers walk free? What is the cost of seeing white mass murderers arrested?*

I have spoken to police who admit that there are bad apples among them, but they are adamant that those cops are a minority. I want to ask, *How many bad apples must there be before you conclude the tree is diseased?*

THE EQUAL JUSTICE INITIATIVE'S (EJI) report on lynching in America notes, "On May 1, 1866, in Memphis, Tennessee, white police officers began firing into a crowd of African American men, women, and children that had gathered on South Street, and afterward white mobs rampaged through Black neighborhoods with the intent to 'kill every Negro and drive the last one from the city.'" Lynchings occurred for decades with full awareness on the part of law enforcement. For the most part, the Black people murdered in public had not committed any crimes. Their infractions were, according to the EJI report, "for minor social transgressions or for demanding basic rights and fair treatment."

These minor social transgressions included not referring to white men as "mister," refusing to move aside for white people in the street, or bumping into a white woman.

THE FIRST TIME I visited South Africa, I stayed overnight with a multi-racial family in Pietermaritzburg, a city in KwaZulu-Natal province. We had gone out to a restaurant for a glass of wine. As we chatted in the falling dusk, one of the family members said, "You know, Megan, fifteen years ago we would have been arrested for sitting at this table with you."

They—would have been *arrested*—for sitting at that table—with *me.*

Seventeen years later, I see what a seismic rupture that statement was: how in one sentence this man had distilled the essence of segregation. How had I managed to make it to age thirty-two without ever being schooled this way? I had grown up learning about the Civil Rights Movement (if I learned about it in school at all) as a historical artifact, a moment calcified, instead of an ongoing, painful struggle in which I too would need to play a part. His words revealed the assumptions at the heart of apartheid and Jim Crow: that people of color endangered white women like me. I would be protected by the rule of law and the presumption of innocence, while they would suffer on my account. Even if all of us were breaking the law (as we would have been, given the Reservation of Separate Amenities Act of apartheid South Africa), they would be the ones to pay.

MICHAEL GERMAN'S report for the Brennan Center, "Hidden in Plain Sight: Racism, White Supremacy, and Far-Right Militancy in Law Enforcement," indicates, "Since 2000, law enforcement officials with alleged connections to white supremacist groups or far-right militant activities have been exposed in Alabama, California, Connecticut, Florida, Illinois, Louisiana, Michigan, Nebraska, Oklahoma, Oregon, Texas, Virginia, Washington, West Virginia, and elsewhere. Research organizations have uncovered hundreds of federal, state, and local law enforcement officials participating in racist, nativist, and sexist social media activity, which demonstrates that overt bias is far too common. These officers' racist activities are often known within their departments, but only result in disciplinary action or termination if they trigger public scandals."

THE CONSTITUTION and Bill of Rights apply to American citizens. Because Black people's citizenship has been contested from the country's founding, whites in power had a convenient rationale for denying them the protections and rights enumerated in the Constitution. In 1740, South Carolina passed the Negro Act, which prevented Black people from owning weapons, among other things: "And for that as it is absolutely necessary to the safety of this Province, that all due care be taken to restrain the wanderings and meetings of Negroes and other slaves, at all times, and more especially on Saturday nights, Sundays, and other holidays, and their using and carrying wooden swords, and other mischievous and dangerous weapons, or using or keeping of drums, horns, or other loud instruments, which may call together or give sign or notice to one another of their wicked designs and purposes; and that all masters, overseers and others may be enjoined, diligently and carefully to prevent the same."

Southern colonies were reluctant to allow Black men to join the military during the Revolutionary War for fear of what armed Blacks might do. I suspect that another, more inarticulate fear was that if Black soldiers fought with honor and courage, whites would have to admit their humanity.

THE OPENING ASSERTION in the Declaration of Independence is *We hold these truths to be self-evident,* meaning that they're so obvious it's hardly worth explaining them. *That all men are created equal. That they are endowed by their Creator with certain unalienable rights.* What must we discern in order to see how empty that promise is and has always been for so many? What have we invested in those lies?

JOHAN TELLS ME that in the mid-1990s in South Africa, after Nelson Mandela's release from prison and the total reorganization of the government, white people were terrified, even more terrified than they had been under apartheid. More so, he thinks, because they were no longer protected by all these presumptions of innocence. They knew apartheid had been indefensible. They were afraid that Black people would kill them, that they would be on the receiving end of the violence they had inflicted for decades.

He says that he senses the same terror here, now.

IT'S SUCH A TELL, this horror of armed Black people in South Africa then, and here in the United States now. It proves, doesn't it? that deep down, white people know perfectly well the privileges they benefit from have nothing to do with their own innate goodness or innocence. They are terrified that what they have done will be visited upon them. And so they lash out with more and more terror-fueled rage, amassing more guns, clinging more desperately to the stories they think will protect them.

April 2023

A grand jury in Akron declines to indict any of the police officers in Jayland Walker's murder.

Depraved Heart; or,
They're Not Injured in Any Way

IN MY MEMORY the edges of the scene are blurred, as if in a dream, though I know I am awake—pitched violently into consciousness from a deep sleep just seconds before. The *crack* that woke me echoes in my skull. Images discolored and stained. Tom sits on the couch. The coffee table has a blackened hole in its center. (Could wisps of smoke still have been streaming from it?) The pistol, on top of the table. Our cherished dog, lying against the wall not four feet away, looking innocently surprised.

I am so out of it, and so confused, that I don't even really understand when he tells me that the gun had gone off. (Not *I shot the gun.* The gun *went off.*)

I say some things, scold him as though he's merely left a faucet dripping. I lurch back to bed. The gravity of his blunder doesn't hit me until the next morning, when I walk into the family room again and the coffee table is gone. Were it not for that strange disappearance, I might have thought that I imagined the whole thing. Surely my husband would not have shot a gun, in our house, in the middle of the night—so close to our beloved dog?

He sends me an email that day, telling me how sorry he is. That he was lucky and stupid at the same time, and that I don't deserve that kind of behavior in my own house.

When I come home from work, he is already there. His face is ashy and stunned.

"I didn't think you would come home today," he tells me. We talk about how stupid he had been not to check whether there was still a bullet in the gun, why he had decided to clean it inside in the middle of the night (had he also been drinking? I wonder, now) with our animals so close by. I tell him that no reproach I could make is as harsh as what he'd impose on himself, and say only that I want him to get rid of the 9mm; he can keep the .30.06 and the .22, but the handgun needs to go. He readily agrees.

Now I wonder if he ever did get rid of it. Once during our divorce, when I had to go back to the house for something, I opened his desk drawer to find a sheet of paper, and there was a gun. Whether it was *the* gun, I don't know.

Altamonte Springs, Florida
August 12, 2021

A toddler in Florida fatally shot a woman during a video call after finding an unsecured handgun, police said Thursday. Someone on the work-related Zoom conference called 911 and reported that they had seen a toddler and heard a noise before the woman, Shamaya Lynn, fell backward, police said. Police said she was the toddler's mother.

Investigators said the handgun belonged to the father of the victim's two young children, the station reported. Neither child was injured.

The case is under investigation, and no charges have been filed.

TOM GREW UP WITH GUNS. He was an Eagle Scout, and taught me to shoot a .22 rifle so that I could kill a rabid animal if I needed to. This was more likely than one might think; we lived on nearly five acres surrounded by national forest, and every year there were reports of attacks on humans by rabid foxes, skunks, even bobcats. I tentatively practiced shooting targets on hay bales at the edge of our property, but I was no good; I figured a lifetime of myopia and corrective lenses had impaired my depth perception. I trusted him, though, when it came to guns. I found his skill sexy, and edgy, proof of the iconoclastic wonky scientist–rugged-outdoorsman persona that I adored about him. I assumed that he was a responsible gun owner.

Cleveland, Ohio
December 23, 2016

Officers responded to Library Avenue near Fulton Road in Cleveland's Clark-Fulton neighborhood at about 10:30 a.m. According to police, a 2-year-old boy shot himself.

The child was taken to nearby MetroHealth Medical Center, where he died from his injuries.

The boy is the son of a 54-year-old Cleveland police officer, Jose 'Tony' Pedro, who was hired in 1993. Cleveland police said the gun was the officer's service weapon.

No arrests have been made.

IT TOOK ME YEARS to realize how dangerous that night really was. As in many other aspects of our life together, I became accustomed to things that would have shocked other people. I never spoke of it to my family or friends until after we divorced, because it had taken on such a weight of shame. Did I really live with a man who fired guns in the house? I started to ask what would have happened if that bullet's trajectory had been even slightly different. What if I had emerged into the hallway to hear my husband shout, "Don't come in here!" What if I had found my dog's blood and brains spattered on the wall behind him? What would that have done to our marriage? What would it have done to me?

I TENTATIVELY told Johan about that night, years later. He stared at me. His response was immediate, unequivocal, and aghast.

"There are certain basic things that you must know and practice if you handle a weapon, and they're not negotiable," he insisted, pounding the edge of his hand onto the opposite palm. "If you park your car on a steep incline, you can't say that you're not going to put on the hand brake. The same goes for a weapon. Anyone with any understanding of a weapon or respect for a weapon will do at least the following when they clean it: inspect it to make sure the safety catch is on, remove the magazine, inspect the chamber to make sure it's empty, inspect it again to make sure it's empty, take it outside, point it at the ground in a safe direction, release the safety catch and fire a dry shot, reengage the safety catch, then start dismantling the gun for cleaning. That's just the absolute basics. All weapons are always loaded. You always have to assume it's loaded. There is no such thing as an unloaded weapon."

His vehemence surprised me. So many steps that I didn't know about; so much naively misplaced faith in Tom's responsibility and awareness. Maybe it was Johan's military training, maybe his temperament, maybe a combination of the two. But for Johan, Tom's "accident" was no accident.

Halifax, Virginia
July 5, 2021

Virginia State Police are investigating a fatal shooting in Halifax that police say appears to be accidental.

The Town of Halifax Police responded to a home in the 5100 block of Halifax Road around 12:45 a.m. Tuesday for a report of a shooting. Officers found a 3-year-old boy with a single gunshot wound. He was taken to Sentara Halifax Regional Hospital, where he died from his injury.

The child's remains are being taken to the Office of Chief Medical Examiner in Roanoke for autopsy.

State police said a handgun was found at the scene. Three adults and a second juvenile were at the home at the time; they were not hurt. No charges have been placed.

IN MY ROLE as an activist with Moms Demand Action for Gun Sense in America, I frequently had to qualify my position by stating that I wasn't against guns, that I didn't want to confiscate them, that I supported the Second Amendment and responsible gun ownership. I had to say this to reassure the people who are terrified that any regulation on guns equals mass confiscation. I had to say this so that I wasn't the one who sounded extreme.

Suffolk, Virginia
July 7, 2021

An 8-year-old accidentally shot and seriously injured a 12-year-old Tuesday, police said.

Suffolk Police said in a news release that the shooting left the 12-year-old with injuries that are serious but aren't thought to be life-threatening.

Police said their preliminary investigation shows the 8-year-old boy got an adult's firearm from a home and accidentally shot the 12-year-old boy.

SPRING 2016 was a particularly bloody season in the United States; in one week in April, four toddlers killed other people with guns. (In 2015, toddlers shot more people in the United States than did terrorists.) From my desk in my sweltering office in South Africa, I read a *Washington Post* story about Jaxon, an Alabama four-year-old, who shot and killed his nine-year-old sister Kimi with a 9mm handgun that their great-grandfather had left out. The reporter recounts pathetic and heartbreaking conversations between Jaxon and his mother, Amanda; Jaxon followed her around the house asking about his "Sissy."

"Why is Sissy not going to feel better?" his mother asks.

"Tell me why," he says.

"Because Sissy died."

"Sissy don't live here anymore?"

"No, Sissy died." (Not *She was shot* and certainly not *You shot her.*)

Sissy died.

AMANDA AND JAXON'S conversation isn't the most horrifying part of the article. That's the paragraph about how Amanda still drives around with a loaded 9mm in the glove compartment of her car, because what if there's an intruder and she needs to protect her remaining child?

Or it's the part where the reporter describes the dozen other guns that the great-grandfather still keeps in the house: "seven pistols and five long guns."

Or it's the line where the reporter casually mentions that the grandfather wasn't charged with any wrongdoing.

I can't decide.

Milwaukee, Wisconsin
May 20, 2021

A 3-year-old boy got a hold of a firearm and unintentionally shot and killed himself in Milwaukee, according to police.

The toddler died Saturday night after shooting himself about 10:30 p.m.

At least eight other children have been killed in Milwaukee shootings so far this year.

MONTHS LATER, I come across an obscure phrase from criminal law: *depraved heart*. It sounds like the title of a tragic romance novel, but its appearance is in connection with the killing of Freddie Gray by Baltimore police officers (*depraved:* from the Latin *de* meaning "down," and *pravare*, "crooked or perverse"). It "establishes that the willful doing of a dangerous and reckless act with wanton indifference to the consequences and perils involved, is just as blameworthy, and just as worthy of punishment, when the harmful result ensues, as is the express intent to kill itself."

Depraved heart murder "suggests that the perpetrator knew the act in question was dangerous and didn't care."

Dekalb County, Georgia
February 12, 2024

A man is in jail facing murder charges after police say a three-year-old boy shot himself in the face.

On Saturday at around 7 a.m., DeKalb County police were called to the 2600 block of Habersham Drive, off Candler Road, regarding a person shot.

When officers arrived, they learned a three-year-old shot himself in the face and his mother had taken him to the hospital where he was pronounced dead.

THIS IS ONE OF THE MANY REASONS why I leave Moms Demand Action; I can't parrot a comforting line to gun owners in order to make reasonable restrictions more palatable. I'm no longer interested in placating paranoid gun owners who refuse to examine their own actions, let alone study any actual research on firearm "accidents" or suicide. I'm more concerned about comforting people whose kids are dead because an adult failed to do the bare minimum to keep a gun away from a child.

I've begun to think that claiming to be a responsible gun owner is like saying you're a responsible tiger owner. *Oh, I keep him penned up. I grew up around tigers so I know what I'm doing. You don't need any training to care for one; anyone knows that. It's my right to have whatever kind of pet I want; the government doesn't get to tell me what to do. No kids can get into his cage. They know not to touch the tiger unless an adult is there. I have a permit. He's for protection.*

The people who trumpet the right to own as many guns as they want, of whatever kind, and to store them however they wish, are often the same people who proclaim the value of personal responsibility over all else. *If you're poor, work harder. If you didn't want that cop to beat you, you shouldn't have been demonstrating. If you didn't want to have sex, you shouldn't have gone to that party in a short dress.* Yet across the states, there is no consistent pattern of holding people responsible for their own deadly failures as gun owners. How is Amanda, the mother in Alabama, permitted to drive with a loaded pistol after losing her own child? How is the grandfather still allowed to own twelve guns after his own recklessness led to his great-granddaughter's murder by her own brother? Why, at the very least, don't people lose the right to own a gun if they leave it loaded and unsecured and a child kills himself?

This is not responsible. That grandfather was not responsible. And American citizens are not responsible as long as we accept that no consequences are appropriate consequences.

That is insane.

East Penn Township, Pennsylvania
June 19, 2020

A family tragedy involving a toddler with a handgun taken from a toy basket has turned into a manslaughter case for the dead 2-year-old-boy's parents.

As WFMZ 69 News reports, the parents are facing felony charges after their son found a loaded Glock 9mm handgun in a living room basket, along with toys and a children's book, then fatally shot himself in the head on Sunday.

When troopers arrived on scene Sunday, they found the boy with a single gunshot to the head in the living room.

They also found a Glock 9mm handgun on the couch with a spent shell casing in the chamber and 17 rounds in the magazine, WFMZ reports, citing court records. Police said the gun's holster didn't have a clasp or any other safety measure and was found in a basket next to the couch with the book and toys.

A search of the house also turned up an AR-15 rifle loaded with 30 rounds of ammunition leaning against a piece of bedroom furniture and a .22 caliber handgun in an unlocked bedroom drawer. The magazine contained 15 rounds of ammunition, WFMZ reports, adding:

[Parents] told troopers they kept the loaded handgun "readily available" for protection when sleeping.

RESPONSIBILITY implies the "ability to respond."

Covington, Virginia
September 12, 2021

A man has been acquitted of charges connected to the death of his son at Lake Moomaw. The trial of Benjamin Jacobsen ended Friday with the jury acquittal in Alleghany Circuit Court. He and his wife, Carrie, were each facing four charges in connection with the death of their toddler son at Lake Moomaw Park in January 2020.

In a revision, all charges were dropped against Carrie Jacobsen, and all but the two dropped against Benjamin before he was acquitted.

At trial, prosecution reviewed evidence that the two-year-old boy had accidentally shot himself after finding a gun under an air mattress.

THE TWENTY CHILDREN murdered at Sandy Hook Elementary School in 2012 are, naturally, the most-remembered victims that day. We would do well, though, to recall that the perpetrator also murdered his mother before embarking on his school rampage: his mother who, in an attempt to connect with him, bought a literal arsenal of weapons and kept them accessible in their home. She bought her guns legally. She practiced and made sure that the killer did, too. She taught him so well that his skills enabled him to murder twenty-seven people and then kill himself.

A responsible gun owner gave an AR-15 Bushmaster to her son, who used it first on her, and then on other people's children.

THE MANCHIN-TOOMEY AMENDMENT, proposed in response to the massacre at Sandy Hook Elementary School, would have required universal background checks on all gun purchases. The Assault Weapons Ban of 2013 was proposed by Dianne Feinstein and twenty-four co-sponsors. Both were defeated in the Senate on April 17, 2013, five days after my shooting.

Manitou Springs, Colorado
July 7, 2021

A 4-year-old child accidentally shot and killed himself while waiting in a car with his mom and sibling, according to Colorado officials. Manitou Springs police responded to a gunshot being fired Tuesday afternoon on Manitou Avenue in Manitou Springs, the El Paso County Sheriff's Office said in a news release. Police said they discovered a 4-year-old child was in a car with his mother and younger sibling when he found a gun and fatally shot himself in the head.

"DEPRAVED HEART" is a poetic term for a fatal disorder. American culture is fundamentally incompatible with gun ownership. This is not to say that all individual gun owners are irresponsible; rather that they, individually, are outliers. As long as there is no nationwide accountability for "negligent" deaths and injuries, no firm and clear consequence to deter anyone from leaving their death tools in reach of children, the bar for "responsible gun ownership" is so low that it is meaningless.

Arming our bodies and our homes demonstrates only that we have concluded that our own lives are worth more than anyone else's. It does not demonstrate responsibility. As a country and a people, our past behaviors—eschewing background checks, blocking gun violence research, allowing people on terrorist watch lists to purchase guns, permitting campus carry, refusing to connect the availability of guns with the inevitability of gun violence—are *dangerous and reckless acts with wanton indifference to the consequences and perils involved.*

Bedford, Virginia
July 5, 2021

People close to one Bedford woman are "heartbroken" after she was shot Saturday and died. 34-year-old Daniel Norwood has been charged with involuntary manslaughter and reckless handling of a firearm. That comes after an incident around 10 p.m. on Burks Hill Road near Liberty Lake Park.

Norwood was in the passenger seat of a vehicle when he allegedly shot 36-year-old Jessica Moore, who was driving.

People close to Moore didn't go on camera Monday, but described her as sweet, smiling and happy.

Bedford police say two children were in the vehicle at the time, but they were not injured.

"So they're not injured in any way. They were returned to their families that night," said Todd Foreman, police chief.

"DEPRAVED HEART" isn't a legal term. It's an epitaph.

You Could Get Raped Every Day; or, Fine People on Both Sides

"Empathy comes from the Greek *empatheia*—em (intro) and *pathos* (feeling)—a penetration, a kind of travel. It suggests you enter another person's pain as you'd enter another country, through immigration and customs, border crossing by way of query: *What grows where you are? What are the laws? What animals graze there?*"

—Leslie Jamison, *The Empathy Exams: Essays*

THE BORDER POST at Rietfontein-Klein Manasse is quiet, remote; the surrounding landscape glitters white on the day we cross from South Africa into Namibia. Johan says that Namibia is called "the land that God forgot." There is a ritual at border control, of course. Officials inspect our *bakkie*, which we've nicknamed Snowball—a sturdy white Nissan four-by-four pickup—we pay ZAR 220, or about fifteen dollars, complete customs forms, hand over our passports for a stamp. I peer at mine with glee when the official slides it back to me. Namibia! In my delight, though, there is a little anxiety. My passport contains a visa for my year in South Africa, but I feel like a trespasser in Namibia, even though I've just been waved in. Am I allowed here, for real? What if I offend someone, make an unforgivable mistake?

Tsau Il Khaeb National Park, once known simply as Sperrgebiet, or "Prohibited Area," is a region on the southwestern coast of Namibia. Even though it's now designated as a park, it's still off-limits to the public, and the diamond company De Beers shares rights to the land with the Namdeb Diamond Corporation. Like coal mining communities in the U.S., diamond miners lived with their families on site, buying necessities from company stores, and, sometimes, smuggling diamonds out via pigeon. Even a forbidden zone can be breached with enough ingenuity.

TWO YEARS AGO, I had gone to a gun show at the Berglund Center in Roanoke, Virginia. Johan was visiting me from South Africa and agreed to come, too. Before becoming a tour guide, Johan had been a major in the South African Air Force, flying C-130s all over Africa. I relied on his military background as a shield and guide to help me understand what I was sure would be utterly alien. I was starting to become more active in writing and speaking out against gun violence, and I often heard people talk about gun shows in tones of hushed disgust. I decided that I needed to go to one, to see what happened there, so that I could speak with more authority. I also thought that by going so far out of my comfort zone, making myself the stranger, I would learn. I had been all over the world, after all; I knew how to be curious, humble, to set aside expectations and simply be present, observe.

We parked our car and as we approached the main entrance, a small cluster of men unwrapped guns on the flatbed of a truck for others' inspection. One man counted out bills and handed them to another, who in turn handed him a long gun. In Virginia, in 2014, if a buyer wished to buy a gun from a federally licensed firearm dealer at a gun show or shop, that seller was required to perform a background check on the buyer. However, private, or face-to-face, gun sales were also permitted at gun shows for which no background check was required.

Johan was aghast. In South Africa, applicants for a gun license (license required) have to give a real reason for why they need a gun; simply "because I want one" isn't enough. The mandatory background checks include employment history, medical and criminal records, and third-party references. Applicants take a firearm safety course and are required to store guns in an approved safe (someone actually comes to your house to check it). You can only buy one gun per license.

There is no legal framework for buying guns out of the back of a truck.

The entry fee was eight dollars. The ticket-taker searched my purse for weapons. Signs everywhere reminded attendees that they were not allowed to carry guns into the center itself. The sale hall was cavernous; from our vantage point at the entry, it looked like a huge swap meet, with tables set end to end. On other days, this venue was the site of high school graduations, musicals, cat shows.

I am not sure what I was expecting, aside from mountains of guns. I'd been to dozens of holiday craft shows in similar settings: tables crowded with crocheted placemats, home-made candles poured into old teacups, jewelry, dog biscuits.

Those were villages I knew, where I could wander carelessly, chat with the residents. Familiar. Safe.

In this village:

Scarlet cloth draped the first display table to our right, which held rows and rows of Nazi memorabilia: flasks, armbands, and medals. Handwritten labels explained the provenance of each one. The table was minded by a bespectacled, white-haired woman wearing a vendor tag. She looked like anyone's grandmother. We tried not to let the shock show on our faces, but I'm sure we failed. (Johan told me later that in South Africa, the public sale of such items violates national hate speech laws and is thus illegal.)

We looked at each other in horror. Neither of us knew what to say. I had expected thousands of guns for sale, and there were, but Nazi relics? Where was I walking? What was this country?

I tried to remember my visits to the Holocaust Museum in Washington, DC, the Museum of the Dutch Resistance and Anne Frank's house in Amsterdam; there must have been Nazi artifacts there, mustn't there? But they weren't for sale. The Holocaust Museum wasn't a marketplace of ideas or goods; there was no equivocation about the moral neutrality of a swastika. I felt for a moment like I did on the day of the shooting, of being in the presence of something so alien and violent that my mind fumbled and blanked. I couldn't fully see it.

We stopped at a table of automatic rifles, among which were several AR-15 Bushmasters, the same kind of gun used to kill twenty first-graders and six teachers at Sandy Hook Elementary School. AR-15s have more than a hundred parts, some with innocuous names like "buffer" and "handguard," words that oddly imply caution. Fully assembled as these are, an AR-15 is all sharp corners and edges; the stock is shaped vaguely like Idaho, the handguard a carapace of concentric rings. It is cold and foreboding. It promises destruction.

On another table were vacuum-packed plastic bags of copper-colored ammunition. Johan murmured that they were hollow-point bullets, used in World War I and subsequently prohibited for use in warfare by the Hague Convention because they are considered too destructive. Some firearms were clearly marketed at female buyers; they were arranged alongside purses with special pockets for concealment, and brightly colored in pink, purple, and turquoise, with female models sporting the guns. Other merchandise included tooled leather wallets and belts, as well as woodwork, jewelry, hats and T-shirts, and military patches.

New swastika flags—not the historical stuff at the first table—were for sale at other tables throughout the hall.

I think we stayed for less than two hours. We didn't talk much on the way home. Neither of us was quite sure where we had been. The people looked like us, the language was the same, but something else was starkly askew. The ground beneath our feet felt unnervingly hollow.

My intention was to learn more about gun enthusiasts and understand why they felt that guns were so central to their lives and identity, but I came away feeling even more alienated than before. I didn't speak to anyone, believing that on this first expedition, observation was best. But I never dreamed that the people there would be selling Nazi shit. I thought about all the baffling, even infuriating things I had encountered in other countries: the awkwardness of eating only with my right hand in Ghana, or older people in South Africa addressing Johan when I'd been the one to pose a question. That was nothing compared to what I'd just seen thirty miles from my own house.

I have to be fair, I thought. *It isn't my culture.* I tried to apply my best logic, reminding myself that other people's choices make perfect sense to them, even if they make no sense to me. But swastikas—that was an uncrossable border. There was no rationalizing that, no way for me to enter into that land and say *well, buying and owning Nazi memorabilia doesn't make you a Nazi.* Even if I hesitated to conclude that the people selling Nazi provenance were themselves Nazis, they didn't disavow Nazi ideology enough to refuse to traffic in its ephemera. The people buying new Nazi items certainly weren't buying in the spirit of historical preservation, were they? How could anyone claim to celebrate the American military (as evident through the sale of other military-style accessories) while at the same time buying *new* Nazi flags?

There was more that troubled me, too. Since Trump became president, I'd heard countless liberal and moderate pundits reminding other liberals and moderates that we had to try and understand where "the other side" was coming from. It's this faith in rational dialogue that ostensibly underpins liberal approaches to social problem-solving, the responsibility to seek common ground. It's one thing to try and understand why people own guns; that feels like a reasonable viewpoint for me to comprehend, even if I might disagree with it.

Nazism, on the other hand, is an impossible bar to clear.

ALONE THIS TIME, I went to another gun show in Salem, Virginia, in 2015. I was prepared to engage with some of the sellers. I had a list of questions and possible follow-ups, which I reviewed in the car beforehand.

The entry ritual was the same as at the previous gun show: entry fee, purse searched, posted reminders that weapons are not allowed. To my untrained eye, a similar variety and quantity of firearms were for sale, though no one was conducting sales from the parking lot. Notably, the Nazi items were missing, but there were plenty of racist products for sale, including T-shirts with President Obama's picture next to a lion, and a caption reading "Lyin' African→African Lion."

I paused at a display case filled with antique guns, things that are too old to use but might have historical significance. One was labeled as having been taken from the body of a German soldier during World War II. I asked the seller about it.

"Yeah," he said. "We're lucky to live in Virginia because I couldn't sell it in Maryland." The seller appraised me. "Are you looking for something in particular?"

"Nope," I said. "Just here to learn."

He eyed me up and down.

"A small woman like you needs to be carrying all the time," he concluded. "Otherwise you leave your husband in a tough position, having to defend you. You have to take responsibility or you could get raped every day."

Raped.

Every day.

"Raped every day?" I asked, incredulous. "So it's my own fault if a man decides to rape me?"

"You've got to take responsibility for yourself," he repeated.

"I've already taken responsibility," I told him.

"Have you ever been in a violent situation?" he asked dubiously.

"Yes, I have."

He shrugged.

"You're still not stepping up," he said. "You can be a wolf, or you can be a sheep."

"There are more choices than that," I told him, and moved on. I didn't stay much longer. I didn't know what to do.

I DON'T REMEMBER the drive home, but it would have taken me on a twisting two-lane road over Catawba Mountain and past the trailhead for McAfee's Knob, one of the most photographed vistas in the Blue Ridge. I don't remember if I thought about how differently you can see from far above, as opposed to down on the ground.

JOURNALIST KAREN ATTIAH, writing in the *Washington Post* in 2022, also encountered this story of rape and guns when she went to a gun show in Texas: "'You can't rape a .38,' one of the gun dealers said, smiling." Gun manufacturers target women in particular, touting guns as the great equalizer, a tool that will cause any would-be rapist to think twice before attacking. "Mama Didn't Raise a Victim," proclaims one ad that shows a young woman wearing ear and eye protection, standing in a field at sundown and holding a pistol in her outstretched hands.

If you get raped, it's your fault. You chose to be a victim. Never mind that your rapist was probably your dad, or uncle, or boyfriend, someone you didn't think you would have to brandish a gun against.

The women at my school who were actually shot—what is wrong with calling them victims? That's what they are. One was working at her desk, the other typing an essay at a computer. A man decided to shoot them. There is no way I can enter a land where their wounds are their fault.

JOHAN had called Namibia the land that God forgot, but I think he/He is wrong. This: my country, the United States, is the forgotten country.

ON OCTOBER 27, 2018, a man with a legally acquired AR-15 and a long social media paper trail of antisemitic and racist posts massacres eleven people in the Tree of Life synagogue in Pittsburgh. I'm out canvassing votes for Virginia's congressional election when the news comes in. I cannot stop crying. I have to abandon the route and go home. *Joyce, Richard, Rose, Jerry, Cecil, David, Bernice, Sylvan, Daniel, Melvin, and Irving.*

In addition to his AR-15, the Pittsburgh shooter had three Glock .357 semiautomatic pistols, also legally acquired. A *New York Times* article reported that he "did not fall into any category barred from gun ownership under federal law, including felons, convicted domestic abusers, dishonorably discharged veterans, or people adjudicated to be mentally ill or subject to certain restraining orders." His social media history, which included phrases like "Jews are the children of Satan," had no impact on his "right" to own guns. Everytown for Gun Safety reports that only twenty-five states prohibit people with hate crime convictions from owning guns.

The Tree of Life massacre was also little more than a year after the Unite the Right rally in Charlottesville, Virginia, where tiki-torch-carrying Nazis marched through the streets chanting "Jews will not replace us" and "Blood and soil!" Johan and I laugh/cried at a sketch Trevor Noah did for the *Daily Show*, where he reminded his American audience that even during apartheid—even when the South African government prohibited Black people from voting—demonstrations by the neo-Nazi Afrikaner Weerstandsbeweging (AWB) group were stopped. Nazism was a bridge too far for even the openly racist apartheid government. But then-president Donald Trump asserted, as we all know now, that "there were very fine people on both sides." "Here's the thing," Noah concluded, "if so many of Trump's supporters are willing to give Nazis the benefit of the doubt, then clearly anything goes. There's no line that they won't cross, and clearly, no cross that they won't burn."

Where have I moved to? Johan asked, after the Charlottesville riot. I had no idea what to tell him.

2019

"She's got Parkinson's," the woman seated behind me hisses. Her friends cackle gleefully in unison.

I do not have Parkinson's. I am shaking my head in disbelief because I'm sitting in a county Board of Supervisors meeting, listening to arguments about the inalienable God-given right to kill oneself and terrify others. Later, at home, I discover that one of the women has pasted a bright orange GUNS SAVE LIVES sticker on the back of my sweater.

Since the Democratic sweep of Virginia's General Assembly in November 2019, and Governor Ralph Northam's proposals for gun reform following a mass shooting in Virginia Beach in May, gun rights advocates have flooded city and county council meetings all over southwestern Virginia to get the counties designated as "Second Amendment sanctuaries." By this, they mean that they hope law enforcement officials will refuse to enforce any new legislation that might abrogate the right to own or carry guns. Tonight, the county sheriff reassures the largely pro-gun crowd that he will never come for a law-abiding citizen's gun.

At the time, my county was partly represented in the legislature by journalist Chris Hurst, whose fiancée Alison Parker, also a local TV journalist, was shot to death on live television in 2015, along with her cameraman. My county has suffered two school shootings: the Virginia Tech massacre, and my own. At the meeting, the Guns Save Lives crowd laughed at shooting survivors and muttered threats at elderly women. They reveled in intimidation and the promise of violence. I cannot comprehend their nihilism. We live in the same county but not the same moral universe. Empathy is impossible when one person's circle of inclusion is wide and another's tiny. How can I empathize with someone who is ready to kill me? What kind of adult pastes a sticker onto a total stranger's back, knowing perfectly well it will hurt her? I can't. I can't.

I won't.

ADAM SERWER wrote an article for *The Atlantic*, just weeks before the Pittsburgh synagogue massacre, about the hideous cruelty of Trump's behavior and policies, titled with the now-viral phrase "The cruelty is the point."

I'VE BEEN WORKING on this memoir for so long, and so frantically, I can't keep pace with the violence. I can't account for every "accidental" shooting, hate-fueled massacre, school shooting, family annihilation. I write and write and read every article that pops up in my Google Scholar alerts. I am so tired. I am so angry. Angry that it's always the responsibility of gun violence prevention activists to constantly live on the defensive and be required, over and over, to justify their perspectives, to "understand" the people who troll gun violence victims online or in real life—or the people who carry Nazi flags. Why must we always do the hard work of understanding *them*? Why are they treated like children who are no more than bullies? Why are they never challenged on their cruelty and hate?

I GO TO A WEEKEND PROGRAM at Yogaville, an ashram in Buckingham County, Virginia, on meditation, compassion, and "managing difficult emotions." Ha. I am not a habitual meditator. It's one of those things that I know would be good for me, and when I do it, I actually feel far steadier, more capacious, but I've never built it into a daily routine.

Like many of the wise women in my life, the teacher, Susan Stone, is an older woman with bright white hair. She teaches mindfulness meditation at the University of Virginia, and she exudes the calm of a still lake surface in winter. I want to be like that; I want my insides to be like my outside. I can't stand the fire that feels like it's literally incinerating my heart from within, when I have to listen to the gun people, when I hear them tell me I'm the crazy one, as though I made him bring a gun to school.

Empathy will burn us out, Dr. Stone tells us. When we try to enter into another person's suffering, we naturally crash up against our own limits. Empathy can't refill us. It's finite. "The meditator is led to reflect on the profound causes of suffering, such as ignorance, which distorts one's perception of reality, or the mental poisons, which are hatred, attachment-desire, and jealousy, which constantly engender more suffering. The process then leads to an increased readiness and desire to act for the good of others."

So many times I've been complimented on my capacity for empathy, and I've felt smugly proud of it, as though it makes me a better victim, as though I haven't let the shooting destroy who I really am. I think of all those gun shows, all those meetings, every rally I've attended, every public speech at which I've been confronted with men carrying guns and a smirk on their faces. I have not thought of them as suffering. But how is it otherwise? The ones at the Board of Supervisors meeting who say *Well, if someone wants to kill themselves they'll find a way, it isn't the gun's fault*—that is suffering. A woman who says I have Parkinson's—Parkinson's!—because I am shaking my head unable to comprehend what I am hearing—this woman who pokes malicious fun at a horrendous disease, and me—she is suffering. The cruelest ones are also suffering and they can't even articulate why.

Roshi Joan Halifax admonishes, in her TED talk, "Moral

outrage is an enemy of compassion." God damn it. What have I been filled with every day for the last years but moral outrage? It has seemed like the only possible response to living in a country where the same slaughter happens every fucking day and nothing changes, where I know that once the blood is mopped up from one crime scene, the headlines will turn again to Congress or Hollywood or Donald Trump and all those deaths, all those lives, will be forced to go on, forgotten.

But what has it gotten me, I have to ask. What has that rage done? Only fed more rage, an ouroboros of flame. Has it helped me heal? Has it given me perspective? Am I a better writer, a better friend or teacher?

I'm not. I have to acknowledge it. I've mistaken empathy for a pure virtue.

So, meditation. I come home from the retreat and set up a tiny shrine on the shelf of an end table. I drape a purple scarf over it so that it's concealed during the day, so that the cats won't bat all my artifacts away. I arrange two LED tea lights, Orthodox icons my parents brought back from Russia, a status of Ganesh my sister brought from India, a smooth stone from the beach at Walvis Bay, in Namibia. A handful of polished stones: labradorite, amazonite, lapis. The prayer book I have copied dozens of invocations into. I sit. For months, for five minutes at a time. I pray the Om Tryamba-kam, the Orthodox Trisagion, Om Namah Shivaya, the Jesus prayer. I try to zero in on this miniature landscape of peace and beauty.

I would be lying if I said I felt an instant shift. It has been more like a faint chipping away, an excavation in miniature. There are only so many directions I can offer my empathy, I see now. The women who mocked me, the gun sellers, the swastika sellers?

I hope they will find an end to their suffering and their fear. I hope they will be able to name their suffering and fear. I hope I will find a country where I can meet them.

Seven Years

In March 2020, as the coronavirus pandemic spread throughout the United States, Americans bought nearly 2 million guns—the second highest monthly total in the decades since such records have been kept.
  —Chana Sacks and Stephen Bartels,
    in *New England Journal of Medicine*

MY YOGA TEACHER told us recently that every seven years, the human body renews itself completely. It's rather lovely to think of inhabiting a fresh body every seven years. Even though we are seven years older, everything is actually brand-new. Untainted. Pure.

Unfortunately, there is no science behind this notion. Our cells divide and regenerate at different rates, so it isn't as though our bodies are engaged in an orderly, efficient seven-year self-cleansing process. We are not new creations; we're that weird house on the corner that always has a pile of shingles in the driveway or a car up on blocks. PERMANENTLY UNDER CONSTRUCTION.

I have learned that trauma doesn't work so efficiently either. It isn't a mechanical, linear system of cleansing and replacement, but a haphazard, unpredictable, messy business full of grinding gears, tension, spinning in place, dizzying shoves forward and back.

April 12, 2020, is the seventh anniversary of my shooting. April 12, 2020, is Easter Sunday.

SEVEN YEARS. This anniversary feels portentous, as though something should be embedded in that number, some lesson that I'm still meant to learn. The number itself is heavy with symbolism: lucky sevens, the Seven Wonders of the Ancient World, a seven-day week in which God rests on that seventh day. Buddha takes seven steps upon being born, and Muslims on the *hajj* circle the Ka'bah seven times. Uranus, the planet representing " radical change, discovery, individuality, and revolution" cycles through our horoscope every seven years. (It is supposed to exit mine at the end of this month; that means it would have entered in March 2013, the month before the shooting.) Even if all my cells haven't newly emerged on their own schedule, I am not the same woman I was on the morning of April 12, 2013. I remember how I spent my afternoon lunch hour googling my ex-husband's affair partner, still fixated on why he had found her so irresistible, why she seemed to be blithely going about her days with no care given to the wreckage that her brief appearance in my life had caused. By two o'clock, she didn't matter at all.

I USED TO BE CONSUMED by laughable hypochondria, to the point that I took myself to the emergency room at twenty-four, convinced that I was having a heart attack. One of my first published essays was about my conviction that every cell in my body was mutating without my knowledge, galaxies of cancer spiraling out of control just under the surface of my skin. I would lie on the beach in late-afternoon sunshine, syrupy warmth soaking into my limbs, and my mind would be filled with images of pinwheeling stars and spirals, a glorious melanoma nebula. Every headache foretold a tumor or an aneurysm.

Cancer geneticist Siddhartha Mukherjee, writing in the *New Yorker*, explores an alternate way to study cancerous metastases: he begins with the zebra and quagga mussels, invasive species that rapidly choked the Great Lakes, though oddly, in their native Ukraine, they remain plodding and innocuous. It is not the mussel that is the sole cause of metastasis; the context, the surrounding ecosystem, is as critical as the mollusk itself. Likewise, in some cancer patients, metastasis occurs years later and kills with ravenous swiftness. In others, metastatic cells might be present, but never flourish to the point that they overpower the healthy tissue. If we use a "seed and soil" metaphor to investigate cancer, Mukherjee writes, "The seed was the cancer cell; the soil was the local ecosystem where it flourished, or failed to. . . . Yet the logic of the seed-and-soil model ultimately raises the question of global ecologies: why does one person's body have susceptible niches and not another's?"

IN JANUARY 2020 I was featured on the radio program "With Good Reason," a production of the Virginia Foundation for the Humanities. The host, Sarah McConnell, asked me a question that no one had ever posed: Why, she inquired, did the shooting continue to cause me so much pain?

I told her that teaching and learning are holy. *Isn't the process of learning a process of change, of admitting that you might be wrong or ignorant or misled?*, I asked, rhetorically. Isn't it a journey of humility, of realizing how small you truly are in the procession of thoughts and lives that have come before you and will succeed you? We ask students to enter a classroom and make themselves vulnerable. A classroom is a crucible for transformation, a garden, not just for our students but for teachers too, and we have to take such care with it. It's precious. We cannot control what our students do with the skills and the knowledge we try to impart to them, but we plant the seeds nonetheless.

My classroom was violated with a shotgun. I can't live with that. I can't just set it aside and pretend that Friday was like any other. It wasn't. It never will be. Like Edna St. Vincent Millay, *I am not resigned.*

IT'S INTRIGUING to read Mukherjee's essay, which was published in 2017, during the spring of 2020. I have been in semi-isolation for more than four weeks now, as the Covid-19 pandemic sweeps across the world. My classes have been moved online; my church is shuttered; my yoga studios are closed; all the places that I would have visited and popped into without a thought require planning to rival a military invasion. Coronavirus eludes scientists' understanding daily. Just a few days ago, a tiger at the Bronx Zoo was diagnosed with it, evidently contracting the virus from an asymptomatic zoo worker. Most zoonoses go the other way. So many mysteries. So many unknowns leaping just ahead of us.

I KNOW THAT THIS YEAR, like the six years preceding it, there will be no newspaper article profiling us, no checkup, no *where-are-they-now*, like there will be only four days later for the anniversary of the Virginia Tech massacre. (And I am proven right: even in the midst of the Covid crisis, all the local TV stations and the newspaper will find space to feature the remembrance of Virginia Tech.) I try not to be bitter that "my" shooting has been forgotten.

I WROTE ONCE that I wished April 12 could be like Leap Day, coming only once every four years, so that I didn't have to dread its arrival every year. I'm not sure I want this anymore. Thinking about April 12 as an "alive day," rather than a bleak anniversary, is a reminder of the precarity of all this, these days, this life—shooter, virus—and yet, I still walk. I see. I breathe.

"IT'S THE SOIL that determines the nature of the illness," Mukherjee writes.

THE WORD "HUMILITY" shares a root with *humus*, the Latin for "earth." I think I must not have had real humility before now. I think of all the times I have cried in my therapist's office, wailing that I would never be okay, fixed, healed, and what was wrong with me that I was so permanently, irreparably damaged by the shooting when everyone else seemed to have moved on.

There is more silver in my hair now, and sometimes when I glimpse myself in a mirror or photograph, I'm taken aback by what looks like a slackness in my cheeks and around the jawline. I wrote once that I felt like I had aged in geologic time, not mere months—as though the very foundations of my being had parched and crumbled. There seemed no life-essence left.

THERE IS ALSO a photograph that my now-husband took of me on August 18, 2015. Just a few hours earlier, he'd pulled off an Oscar-worthy proposal on a commercial flight from Johannesburg to Cape Town. With the help of the pilot (an old Air Force buddy), the second officer, an entire cabin crew, and the security and logistics team of Lanseria Airport, he'd gotten on the PA system from the cockpit, requested the permission of the passengers to "ask a special lady an important question," and emerged bearing an embarrassed grin and a gorgeous diamond solitaire.

In the photo, I am sitting with my arm around the statue of a Great Dane named Just Nuisance, an honorary member of the South African Navy, who was given a full military burial upon his death. We are in the oceanside hamlet of Simon's Town, just an hour or so up the coast from Cape Town. The sun is shining in my eyes, which are dark and crinkled against the light. My smile is most striking; I don't like to smile broadly in pictures, preferring instead a closed-lip smirk. In this picture, though, I am wearing the most natural and open smile I think I have ever worn. I am sitting next to a statue of an enormous dog, on the seaside, in the beloved country, now the fiancée of a man whose integrity, courage, and loyalty transcend any I have ever known. Yes, to trying again. Yes, to Africa. Yes, to learning. Yes, to love.

As I WRITE THIS, I am under a stay-at-home order from the governor's office. There are more than a million diagnosed cases of Covid-19, or coronavirus, around the world, and the United States has overtaken Italy and China as the global epicenter of the disease. Just today, the CDC designated Virginia as a state in which there's a high rate of community transmission. For the past three weeks I have left the house only to walk my dog and to go to the supermarket, which I schedule once a week. In the aisles at Wal-Mart and Kroger, people walk furtively with scarves wrapped around their faces or a precious medical mask tied around the backs of their heads.

It is a surreal thing, to write this in the midst of a pandemic. I read anecdotes online that people who have already survived trauma are managing far better than others; on her Instagram feed, writer Kelly Sundberg reflects, "When chaos is what we know, it's already familiar." I have friends who are driving themselves mad trying to disinfect every doorknob and surface in their homes, who hold their breath when they go outside to fetch the mail. I read their texts and can feel my forehead wrinkle in bafflement, wondering if there's so much more that I ought to be doing with my day. But my friend whose son shot himself three months ago today texted me, "We know control is an illusion."

It's a gift, this: but oh, the price of receiving it is so desperately high. At the same time that I don't want anyone else to ever have to experience what I have, I cannot deny the freedom that it's given me, the courage to uproot my life and move to South Africa for a year; to marry and risk all that comes with love and marriage; to write a book that contains all the terror and grief and joy that's come in the last seven years.

Resurge: rise again. The root of "resurrection."

IN NINE DAYS, it will be Easter.

EVERY CELL ANEW, seven years later.

AT THIS MOMENT, I am alive, and no one is shooting. At this moment, there is just breath, April sun on the lilacs, and stillness.

More Present than Hope

IN AUGUST 2023, hundreds of seekers descended on Loch Ness, Scotland, in the largest and most organized search for the legendary Nessie in fifty years. A photo taken in 2018 has just surfaced (pun intended) seeming to reveal dual humps, the newest photographic "evidence" of this mystery that continues to grip public imagination. It makes me remember my field trip there in 1996, when I was a college junior, what seems like a lifetime ago.

PEOPLE CONTINUE TO ASK, in interviews and in private conversations, what I feel hopeful about when it comes to gun violence prevention. Sometimes, though, when I think of the galaxy of violence, I remember the scene in *A Wrinkle in Time* where Meg watches a star sacrifice itself to an amoral, amorphous force of destruction, the Dark Thing: "The Darkness seemed to seethe and writhe. Was this means to *comfort* them?"

I TOLD MY STUDENTS this semester that words are like geodes; you can split them apart and excavate their component parts, the glittery Germanic or Romantic or Indigenous root that gives clues to the word's ancient meaning.

Of course, I do know about the etymological fallacy: the false assumption that a word's roots point to its true meaning, rendering the current one incorrect. That is not what I am getting at. What I mean is: the aftermath of violence stole language from me. Words had never failed me until the shooting, when all the frantic research I conducted left me despondent. And words like *safe*, *hope*, *change*, *protect* no longer mean what I thought they did. I've been confronted with people literally wearing guns on their backs telling me that they're the protectors of us all, told that unless I carry a gun I deserve to be raped. I had no idea that another human being and I could utter and interpret the same word so differently—even *differently* isn't strong enough a word. As though we are not using the same word at all, as though we are not speaking the same language. So, the roots: I am going back to the roots to see how this all fits together, if it all fits together.

SOMEONE I WORK WITH and admire in the gun violence prevention sphere, whose child was shot in a well-known massacre, says that this work is a marathon, not a sprint. I try to tell myself that this very week, when a professor at the University of North Carolina is murdered in his office by a graduate student. It has been more than fifteen years since this activist's child was shot, more than ten since my shooting. In those intervening years Congress has refused to act on so many occasions I can't even count. To wait, indeed. Hope and waiting are so entangled in my mind that I can hardly separate them. How long can anyone be expected to keep up hope when they see over and over again the same mistakes, the same bloodshed? Hope does indeed feel like a mystery, a word of unknown origin.

LOCH NESS is twenty-three miles long and seven hundred fifty-five feet deep at its lowest point; the Washington Monument could be completely submerged in it, with another two hundred feet to spare. The water is tea-colored and murky from the vast amount of peat floating in it. It is not hard for me to imagine something living in there that has, so far, chosen its moments of self-revelation carefully. The earliest sighting of Nessie was in the sixth century, in a biography of St. Columba. As the lacustrine beast attacked another monk, Columba "stepped forward boldly to the edge of the loch and, making the sign of the cross while invoking the Name of the Lord, spoke in a commanding voice. 'You will go no further!'"

Is there a through-line from the children to the adults with a secret fascination with cryptids like Nessie (cryptid: from Greek *kryptos*, hidden)? I can still picture the shelf in my elementary-school library where an oversize book on UFOs, monsters, and myths lived. I checked it out God knows how many times; in middle school, when I went back to visit my favorite teachers, I could pick that book off the shelf and see my childish second-grade cursive still on the card tucked inside. As an adolescent, I repeatedly checked out an oversize photography book called *Unicorns I Have Known* from the public library. Photographs, I thought, not illustrations, must prove that unicorns are real! I wonder if part of the allure of the unicorn is its adjacency to something as familiar as horses.

It's just strange enough to seem possible. Narwhals are real, after all. Nature quirks in all kinds of ways; what's to stop it from placing a graceful horn atop a horse's noble brow?

SOMETIMES as an icebreaker, on the first day of class, we talk about our dream jobs. Flower shop owner comes up a lot. Panda handler. TikTok star. Blacksmith. For me, it's crypto-zoologist. I have a handbook of cryptids on the shelf as well as a U.S. map with illustrations of various state monsters. Mothman. Champ. The Michigan Dogman. In his book *The Unidentified: Mythical Monsters, Alien Encounters, and Our Obsession with the Unexplained*, Colin Dickey remarks, "Much of what attracts people to these fringe beliefs is a belief in a world of wonder and marvel, a world outside the ken of humanity, a world just out of reach." I would like to think that I'm not one of the crazy conspiracy theorists who believe in QAnon and the deep state; my beliefs in Nessie and Sasquatch and the *mokele-mbembe* (an extant dinosaur-ish creature said to live in the Congolese jungle) are benevolent, fueled by childish wonder. I love the idea that in the craggy Himalaya there might be a yeti (because Peter Matthiessen, in his 1978 memoir *The Snow Leopard*, mentions an isolated monastery that possesses a painting of a female yeti). In the depths of so many lakes around the world, maybe there is a dinosaur-fish-creature that bides its time, waits for the opportune moment to surface and take a breath—maybe. It doesn't matter if I never see one, or if there's no solid quantifiable evidence to prove it exists. Haven't human beings been wrong on scores of things, haven't we demonstrated the degrees of our cocky arrogance? Wouldn't the world be better if all those creatures were real? Sometimes when I can't sleep, I imagine all these creatures, in their mountain heights or forests or lakes, peaceful, unbothered. Just there. Just alive.

"WHAT PEOPLE ARE SEEKING in cryptids is their own escape from the world of humans from which they come," writes Dickey.

A WOMAN OPENED FIRE at megachurch preacher Joel Osteen's church in Houston on February 11, 2024. A woman this time, unusual: but like so very, very many other shooters, she used an AR-15. Like so very, very many other shooters, too, she had a long history of arrests and had been subject to an emergency detention order. Family members had alerted Child Protective Services, fearing for her mental state; she evidently carried a gun in her child's diaper bag. Her seven-year-old son was with her at the shooting. He was shot in the head and has sustained critical injuries, according to other family members.

The boy's name is Samuel, meaning "name of God" or "God has heard."

IN *A WRINKLE IN TIME*, just as they are about to travel, or tesser, through the Dark Thing, the sage? angel? messenger? Mrs. Whatsit admonishes Meg, "Stay angry, little Meg. You will need all your anger now."

BELIEVE ME, I want to tell the people who ask me about hope that there is a reason for it, that change will come and one day they will send their kids to school without fear. I want to be able to give them good news. I wish I could give them something because I can see that people yearn for it. I suspect that even the most hysterical gun nuts, deep down, are petrified of what they have unleashed and they just don't know how to roll it back; they don't have the language or the social capital or the fortitude to withstand the loss of face they might experience. Sometimes I can even muster a little sympathy for them, imagining what it must be like to go through life so afraid. They wouldn't call it fear, I suspect, but if you've structured your entire life around the "right" to kill someone who scares you, what is at the core but terror?

"HOPE is not prognostication," wrote Václav Havel. "It is an orientation of the spirit, an orientation of the heart; it transcends the world that is immediately experienced, and is anchored somewhere beyond its horizons." This reminds me that hope may be like love; it is not an emotion but an action, a choice. Hope: waiting, enduring.

ON CONSPIRACY BELIEFS, Dickey writes, "Much of this is driven by what's sometimes called apophenia, the tendency to see shapes and patterns where none exist. This apophenic perception lies at the heart of many fringe beliefs and conspiracy theories—it is the idea that everything is, one way or another, connected."

I know apophenia. I first learned the word in David Morris's *The Evil Hours: A Biography of Post-Traumatic Stress Disorder*. It explains why I am coolly convinced that I will one day be shot, probably killed: how else to account for the tightening noose of my proximity to gun violence? Dunblane to Columbine to Virginia Tech to my own school: the only thing left is for a bullet to pierce my body. It already lives in my mind and soul.

And isn't the idea that everything is connected also a spiritual one, a caution or reminder that whatever we do or say has ethereal echoes that we can't foresee? None of us is a universe of one. That is the heart of the southern African concept of *ubuntu*, the notion that there is no me without you. We are human because of, and with, other people. The refusal to accept that connectedness inflames gun apologists who insist that *your feelings don't trump my rights*. What if life itself is endless apophenia, if only we have the courage to see it?

SO, PATTERNS: At the end of September 2023, California Governor Gavin Newsom signed new laws that strengthened concealed-carry rules and taxed ammunition.

On October 1, 2023, new gun laws took effect in Connecticut. Signed by Governor Ned Lamont in June, they prohibit open carrying of firearms and limit the number of guns one can buy in a month.

In May 2023, the Roanoke, Virginia NAACP hosted another "Groceries, Not Guns" gun buyback, where people turn in firearms in exchange for gift cards: $250 for a handgun and $150 for rifles, revolvers, or shotguns. Earlier events yielded over two hundred fifty guns purchased and destroyed. My friend Catherine, who's one of the coordinators, called it "a divestment from a culture of guns and violence and investment in a culture of nonviolence and community."

Hope is a choice.

And yet: Today, October 5, 2023, this was in the *New York Times*: "[A]ccording to an analysis published on Thursday, the rate of firearm fatalities among children under 18 increased by 87 percent from 2011 through 2021 in the United States. The death rate attributable to car accidents fell by almost half, leaving firearm injuries the top cause of accidental death in children. The finding underscores additional data showing that firearm injuries are now the leading cause of death among Americans under 20, after excluding deaths of infants born prematurely or with congenital abnormalities." The article notes that a spokesman for the National Shooting Sports Foundation said, "The firearms industry does not oppose design features that would make guns childproof but does oppose mandates to introduce such features."

Patterns: October 25, 2023. Lewiston, Maine, this time. Eighteen murdered in a bowling alley and restaurant. February 20, 2024. Kansas City, Missouri, at a Super Bowl parade. One killed, twenty-two wounded.

We writing instructors are always reminding students to think of their audience, consider the readers' needs: their assumptions, their knowledge gaps—but at the same time that I am writing this book, I am writing to try and convince myself that a different world is possible. It is so hard. It is so impossible. The Loch Ness Monster is more real to me sometimes, more present, than hope for change. What I believe in now is possibility.

I can only imagine how hard it is to dive in Loch Ness, to find one's way in the midst of that cold, silty water that lets so little light through. Maybe she is in there, finding her way as she and her kin have for centuries. I cannot think of a better metaphor for my life since the shooting, trying to orient myself in a world that is both familiar and alien, peering through the dark, aiming for the light.

Notes

EPIGRAPH

ix ***By their laughter I know my students:*** Lucinda Roy, *No Right to Remain Silent: What We've Learned from the Tragedy at Virginia Tech* (New York: Three Rivers Press, 2009), xx.

PROLOGUE

3 ***An article in* Smithsonian *magazine:*** Meilan Sholly, "How the 1996 Dunblane Massacre Pushed the U.K. to Enact Stricter Gun Laws," *Smithsonian*, March 12, 2021.

3 ***In April 2013, mere months after the massacre:*** Ted Barrett and Tom Cohen, "Senate rejects expanded gun background checks," April 18, 2013, https://www.cnn.com/2013/04/17/politics/senate-guns-vote/index.html.

4 ***The word hope:*** https://www.etymonline.com/word/hope.

DOORS

11 ***This is not really, this this this is not really happening.*** Tori Amos, "Cornflake Girl," (1993).

SOUTH AFRICA: THE BEGINNING

20 ***What did I know about the fifty-five (give or take) countries of Africa?:*** Alexandra Fuller, *Leaving Before the Rains Come* (New York: Penguin, 2016).

20 ***She had always wanted words:*** Michael Ondaatje, *The English Patient* (New York: Alfred A. Knopf, 1992).

21 *Without sentimentality or foolish regrets:* Trevor Huddleston, *Naught for Your Comfort* (Garden City, NY: Doubleday, 1956).

22 *A police spokesman in Pretoria: New York Times*, February 14, 1984.

26 *The word "museum":* https://www.etymonline.com/search?q=museum

SANCTUARY

35 *Three years I had there:* Spencer Reece, "Sanctuary," *The Clerk's Tale* (Boston: Houghton Mifflin, 2004).

39 *Research from Harvard's School of Public Health:* Harvard T. H. Chan School of Public Health, Injury Control Research Center, "Homicide" and "Suicide."

40 *In the West, it was believed:* Alexandra Fuller, *Leaving Before the Rains Come* (New York: Penguin Press, 2015).

SOUTH AFRICA: THE MIDDLE

43 *Migratio, Latin:* https://www.etymonline.com/word/migration

47 *There are three kinds of memory loss:* Antjie Krog, *Country of My Skull: Guilt, Sorrow, and the Limits of Forgiveness in the New South Africa* (New York: Times Books, 1999).

48 *Dr. Gobodo-Madikizela does not sugarcoat the commission's shortcomings:* David Marchese, "What Can Americans Learn from South Africa about National Healing?" *New York Times*, December 11, 2020.

49 *In this article, Carlson recounts:* Jennifer D. Carlson, "From a Society of Survivors to a Survivor Society," *Footnotes: A Magazine of the American Sociological Association* 50, no. 4.

49 *Dr. Gobodo-Madikizela reminds her interviewer:* David Marchese, "What Can Americans Learn from South Africa?"

51 *We, the people of South Africa:* https://www.gov.za/documents/constitution/constitution-republic-south-africa-1996-04-feb-1997.

51   ***What we find exotic abroad:*** Alain de Botton, *The Art of Travel* (New York: Pantheon, 2002).

BY MY OWN HAND

54   ***A thorough crisis is a death experience:*** James Hillman, *Suicide and the Soul* (New York: Harper & Row, 1964).

55   ***I go to new river community college:*** David Kravets, "Virginia Mall Shooter Apparently Announced Crime in Advance on 4chan," Wired.com, April 12, 2013.

55   ***Rachel Kalish and Michael Kimmel assert:*** Rachel Kalish and Michael Kimmel, "Suicide by Mass Murder: Masculinity, Aggrieved Entitlement, and Rampage School Shootings," *Health Sociology Review* 19, no. 4 (2010): 451–64.

56   ***When departs the fierce soul from the body:*** Dante Alighieri, *The Divine Comedy: The Vision of Hell, or The Inferno*, canto 13, 1317. http://www.public-domain-poetry.com/dante-alighieri/divine-comedy-by-dante-the-vision-of-hell-or-the-inferno-canto-xiii-14130

61   ***A suicide may leap free of another's judging:*** Margaret Gibson, "Judge Not," *Image*, no. 106 (2020).

61   ***I look up the etymology of the word "lament:"*** https://www.etymonline.com/search?q=lament

62   ***It is useful to remember that suicide can be a search for meaning:*** David Lester, "Suicide as a Search for Spirituality," *American Journal of Pastoral Counseling* 1, no. 2 (1998).

63   ***Transformation begins at this point:*** James Hillman, *Suicide and the Soul.*

MEN APPEAR TO ME AS MONSTERS

66   ***A sense of loss so huge and irreparable:*** Jon Krakauer, *Into the Wild* (New York: Anchor Books, 1997).

67   ***They fled their home on East Street:*** Lisa Miller, "A Handgun for Christmas," NYMag.com, July 18, 2022.

67   ***I need not describe the feelings:*** Mary Shelley, *Frankenstein, or the Modern Prometheus* (1818).

68   *According to a prosecutor's motion:* Lisa Miller, "A Handgun for Christmas."

69   *Perhaps the immutable error of parenthood:* Andrew Solomon, *Far from the Tree: Parents, Children and the Search for Identity* (New York: Scribner's, 2013).

70   *"Monster" comes from a Latin root:* https://www.etymonline.com/search?q=monster

70   *Like all mythologies, this belief that Dylan was a monster:* Sue Klebold, *A Mother's Reckoning: Living in the Aftermath of Tragedy* (New York: Crown, 2016).

72   *Andrew Solomon asks Peter Lanza about his son's funeral:* Andrew Solomon, "The Reckoning," *New Yorker*, March 10, 2014.

73   *I'll lend you for a time a little child of mine:* Edgar A. Guest, "A Child of Mine," 1930.

SECURITY THEATER

75   *It is fear that rules this land:* Alan Paton, *Cry, the Beloved Country* (New York: Scribner's, 1948).

76   *The officers waited, the report found:* J. David Goodman and Edgar Sandoval, "Report on Uvalde Shooting Finds 'Systemic Failures' in Police Response," *New York Times*, July 17, 2022.

77   *The [Uvalde] district said it was fortifying campuses:* Edgar Sandoval, "'I Don't Feel Safe': Children Fear Going Back to School in Uvalde," *New York Times*, August 23, 2022.

80   *Security comes from Latin, securus:*

80   *Sanctuary: "consecrated place; place of refuge or protection:"* https://www.etymonline.com/search?q=sanctuary

80   *The bags must be completely clear:* Ayana Archie, "Students in a Dallas school district must wear clear backpacks after Uvalde shooting," NPR, July 19, 2022.

80   *The Department of Homeland Security allocated:* Carole Levine, "Teaching Kids to Treat Wounds in School Shoot-

ings: Putting Band-Aids on the Real Issues," *Nonprofit Quarterly*, December 18, 2018.

80 **. . . *during a mass casualty event, a security officer thought:*** Robert Snell, "Oxford security guard didn't stop shooting, thought dying student was covered in makeup: lawyer," *Detroit News*, August 3, 2022.

81 ***a bulletproof backpack manufacturer:*** About Us, TuffyPacks.com.

82 ***The New York Times published a long article:*** Sarah Mervosh, "Trained, Armed, and Ready to Teach," *New York Times*, August 5, 2022.

84 ***Today is March 19, 2024:*** https://www.gunviolencearchive.org.

TO THE THIRD AND FOURTH GENERATIONS

87 ***Historical trauma . . . is the "incomplete mourning and resulting depression absorbed by children":*** Bonnie Duran, Eduardo Duran, and Maria Yellow Horse Brave Heart, "Native Americans and the Trauma of History," in *Studying Native America: Problems and Prospects in Native American Studies* (Madison: University of Wisconsin Press, 1998).

87 ***If "the body keeps the score":*** Bessel van der Kolk, *The Body Keeps the Score: Brain, Mind, and Body in the Healing of Trauma* (New York: Viking, 2014).

91 ***In the 20 years since Columbine:*** Jared Keller, "The Psychological Aftermath of Surviving School Shootings," *Pacific Standard*, March 25, 2019.

91 ***"catastrophic expectancy":*** Natan P. Kellermann, "Transmission of Holocaust Trauma: An Integrative View," *Psychiatry Interpersonal and Biological Processes* 64, no. 3 (2001): 256–67.

92 ***One of the witnesses said:*** Editorial board, *Denver Post*, March 23, 2021.

92   *"It is, perhaps, the fatal flaw:"* David J. Morris, *The Evil Hours: A Biography of Post-Traumatic Stress Disorder* (Boston: Houghton Mifflin Harcourt, 2015).

"SWEET, QUIET BOYS;" OR, DIVINITIES IMPLACABLE

94   *"We are gratified:"* Molly Hennessy-Fiske, Matt Pearce, & Jenny Jarvie, "Texas school shooter killed girl who turned down his advances and embarrassed him in class, her mother says," *Los Angeles Times,* May 19, 2018.

94   *I take the word apart like a surgeon:* https://www.etymonline.com/search?q=annihilate

94   *Family annihilations happen every five days:* Nancy Molnar, Amy L. Knapp, and Jeanine Santucci, "Family shot to death, including three young children, in quadruple murder-suicide in Ohio," USAToday Network, August 25, 2023.

95   *South African writer and scholar Njabulo Ndebele:* Pumla Dineo Gqola, "'The Difficult Task of Normalizing Freedom': Spectacular Masculinities, Ndebele's Literary/Cultural Commentary, and Post-Apartheid Life," *English in Africa* 36, no. 1 (May 2009).

95   *I was having a bad week:* "NRV Mall shooting suspect in court," WSET.com, April 15, 2013.

96   *[Murderer's name] . . . was always kind and good to us:* Shannon Watts on X, January 14, 2023. Posts on the funeral home's website were deleted.

97   *Malign Tisiphone seized a torch steeped in blood:* https://www.theoi.com/Khthonios/Erinyes.html.

99   *"I concluded that women are flawed":* Elliot Rodger, "My Twisted World," 2014, https://www.nytimes.com/interactive/2014/05/25/us/shooting-document.html.

99   *No prayer, no sacrifice, and no tears can move [the Furies]:* https://www.theoi.com/Khthonios/Erinyes.html.

100   *In the Metamorphoses:* https://ovid.lib.virginia.edu/trans/Metamorph4.htm#478205201.

JUST ANOTHER WEEK IN 2022

103 *a conspiracy theory that states that nonwhite individuals are being brought into the United States:* Dustin Jones, "What is the 'great replacement' and how is it tied to the Buffalo shooting suspect?" NPR, May 16, 2022.

104 *It is our firm belief that God's purpose for our company:* https://www.intercape.co.za/who-we-are/.

104 *In the United States, white people are 61 percent of the population:* US Census Bureau, "Race and Ethnicity in the United States: 2010 Census and 2020 Census," https://www.census.gov/library/visualizations/interactive/race-and-ethnicity-in-the-united-state-2010-and-2020-census.html.

104 *It's this resentment that connects him:* James Pogue, "Letter from South Africa: The Myth of White Genocide," *Harper's Magazine*, March 2019.

105 *It is not crime that matters. It is control.:* Huddleston, *Naught for Your Comfort.*

106 *Surely if the incarnation means anything at all:* Huddleston, *Naught for Your Comfort.*

108 *The key variable in the way that the Second Amendment operates:* Carol Anderson, *The Second: Race and Guns in a Fatally Unequal America* (New York: Bloomsbury, 2021).

109 *On May 1, 1866, in Memphis, Tennessee, white police officers began firing:* Equal Justice Initiative, *Lynching in America: Confronting the Legacy of Racial Terror*, 3rd ed. (2017). https://lynchinginamerica.eji.org/report.

110 *Since 2000, law enforcement officials with alleged connections:* Michael German, "Hidden in Plain Sight: Racism, White Supremacy, and Far-Right Militancy in Law Enforcement," Brennan Center for Justice, 2020.

111 *In 1740, South Carolina passed the Negro Act:* https://ushistoryscene.com/article/excerpts-south-carolina-slave-code-1740-no-670-1740/.

DEPRAVED HEART; OR, THEY'RE NOT INJURED IN ANY WAY

114 *Altamonte Springs, Florida:* Phil Helsel, "Toddler shoots, kills mom during video call after finding gun," NBC News, August 12, 2021.

115 *Cleveland, Ohio:* Jack Shea, "2-year-old son of Cleveland police officer dies after shooting self," FOX8, December 23, 2016.

117 *Halifax, Virginia:* Sarah Irby, "Police: Toddler accidentally shot and killed himself," WDBJ7, July 6, 2021.

118 *Suffolk, Virginia:* "8-year-old accidentally shot 12-year-old in Suffolk, police say," WSLS10 News, July 7, 2021.

118 *Why is Sissy not going to feel better?:* Terrence McCoy, "After a toddler accidentally shot and killed his older sister, a family's wounds run deep," *Washington Post*, December 1, 2016.

119 *Milwaukee, Wisconsin:* Associated Press, "Three-year-old dies after accidentally shooting himself," *US News & World Report*, May 10, 2021.

120 *It "establishes that the willful doing of a dangerous and reckless act . . .":* Lily Rothman, *Time*, May 1, 2015.

120 *DeKalb County, Georgia:* Bryan Mims, "Brother charged after 3-year-old shoots, kills himself in DeKalb County," WSB-TV, February 12, 2024.

122 *East Penn Township, Pennsylvania:* John Luciew, "Pa. parents charged with manslaughter after son, 2, shoots himself in head with gun from 'toy basket,'" PennLive *Patriot-News*, May 29, 2020.

123 *Covington, Virginia:* "Father acquitted of child's death at Lake Moomaw," WDBJ7, September 13, 2021.

124 *Manitou Springs, Colorado:* Summer Lin, "4-year-old shoots himself in front of mom and sibling in car, Colorado officials say," *Sacramento Bee*, July 7, 2021.

125 *Bedford, Virginia:* Michael Alachnowicz, "People close to Bedford woman fatally shot Saturday are 'heartbroken,'" WDBJ7, July 5, 2021.

YOU COULD GET RAPED EVERY DAY; OR, FINE PEOPLE ON BOTH SIDES

126 *Empathy comes from the Greek empatheia:* Leslie Jamison, *The Empathy Exams: Essays* (Minneapolis: Graywolf Press, 2014).

133 *You can't rape a .38:* Karen Attiah, "I asked about abortion at a Texas gun show. The answer I got was grim," *Washington Post,* July 11, 2022.

134 *[H]e did not fall into any category barred from gun ownership:* Source: Robert Oppel, "Synagogue Suspect's Guns Were All Purchased Legally, Inquiry Finds," *New York Times,* October 30, 2018.

135 *"Here's the thing," Noah concluded:* https://www.cc.com/video/ahxcur/the-daily-show-with-trevor-noah-trump-s-troublesome-response-to-the-charlottesville-violence, August 21, 2017.

137 *Serwer wrote an article for* **The Atlantic:** Adam Serwer, "The Cruelty Is the Point," *The Atlantic,* October 3, 2018.

138 *The meditator is led to reflect:* Matthieu Ricard, "From Empathy to Compassion in a Neuroscience Laboratory," https://info-buddhism.com/Empathy-Compassion-Neuroscience-Ricard-Altruism.html 2015.

138 *Moral outrage is an enemy of compassion:* Roshi Joan Halifax, "Compassion and the True Meaning of Empathy," TED.com, July 14, 2015.

SEVEN YEARS

141 *[A]s the coronavirus pandemic spread, . . . Americans bought nearly 2 million guns:* Chana Sacks and Stephen Bartels, "Reconsidering risks of gun ownership and suicide in unprecedented times," *New England Journal of Medicine,* June 3, 2020.

142 *Uranus, the planet representing:* Larry Schwimmer, "The reason we experience major life & relationship changes every 7 years," *Elephant Journal,* October 13, 2017.

143 *The seed was the cancer cell:* Siddhartha Mukherjee, "Cancer's Invasion Equation," *New Yorker,* September 4, 2017.

144 *I am not resigned:* Edna St. Vincent Millay, "Dirge Without Music," in *Collected Poems* (1928).

145 *The word "humility:"* https://www.etymonline.com/search?q=humility

MORE PRESENT THAN HOPE

149 *In August 2023, hundreds of seekers descended on Loch Ness:* Dustin Jones, "Monster hunters are conducting the largest search of Loch Ness in more than 50 years," NPR, August 21, 2023.

149 *The Darkness seemed to seethe and writhe:* Madeleine L'Engle, *A Wrinkle in Time* (New York: Farrar Straus, 1962).

151 *Columba "stepped forward boldly to the edge of the loch":* Angelo Stagnaro, "St. Columba and the Loch Ness Monster," *National Catholic Register*, November 25, 2018.

152 *Much of what attracts people to these fringe beliefs:* Colin Dickey, *The Unidentified: Mythical Monsters, Alien Encounters, and Our Obsession with the Unexplained* (New York: Viking, 2020).

152 *an isolated monastery that possesses a painting of a female yeti:* Peter Matthiessen, *The Snow Leopard* (New York: Viking, 1978).

153 *A woman opened fire:* J. David Goodman, Edgar Sandoval, and Ruth Graham, "Houston Megachurch Shooter Had an AR-15 and Brought Her 7-Year-Old Son," *New York Times*, February 12, 2024.

153 *Samuel:* https://www.thebump.com/b/samuel-baby-name.

153 *Stay angry, little Meg:* Madeleine L'Engle, *A Wrinkle in Time.*

154 *Hope is not prognostication:* Václav Havel, *Disturbing the Peace* (New York: Vintage Books, 1991).

155 *California governor Gavin Newsom signs laws:* Hannah Wiley, "Newsom signs gun laws that add new taxes and limit where owners can carry firearms," *Los Angeles Times*, September 26,

2023.

155 **On October 1, 2023, new gun laws take effect in Connecticut:** Office of Legislative Research, Public Act Summary, https://www.cga.ct.gov/2023/sum/pdf/2023SUM00053-R02HB-06667-SUM.pdf.

155 **In May 2023, the Roanoke, Virginia NAACP hosted:** Isabella Ledonne, "Roanoke prepares for another gun buyback event; turn guns in for groceries," WDBJ7, May 19, 2023.

155 **[A]ccording to an analysis published on Thursday:** Roni Caryn Rabin, "Gun Deaths Rising Sharply Among Children, Study Finds," *New York Times*, October 5, 2023.

Acknowledgments

I would like to thank so many people and institutions.

Caroline Bock and everyone at Washington Writers' Publishing House, for championing this book from beginning to end. Thank you.

The many friends who have held me up and believed in this project: Anne, Christine, Dana, Elizabeth, Jackie, Jen, Kristen, Latanya, Leanna, Manisha, Melissa, Robyn, Susan L., Susan W., Susie, Tavi, and Tracy.

New River Community College, for the gift of sabbatical leave and such enviable colleagues.

The Department of English at the University of the Free State, for giving me space and time to write.

Jo and Nelson Evans, for sanctuary.

The Yogaville community in Buckingham, Virginia, for being such a haven of kindness.

The community of Asbury United Methodist Church, for the same.

My family, particularly my parents, for their care of my beloved animals while I was across the world.

Washington Writers' Publishing House is a non-profit, cooperative literary organization that has published over 100 volumes of poetry since 1975 as well as fiction and nonfiction. The press sponsors three annual competitions for writers living in DC, Maryland, and Virginia, and the winners of each category (one each in poetry, fiction, and creative nonfiction) comprise our annual slate. In 2021, WWPH launched an online literary journal, WWPH WRITES to expand our mission to further the creative work of writers in our region. In 2024, WWPH launched our biennial works in translation series. More about the Washington Writers' Publishing House at www.washingtonwriters.org

9 781941 551417